16.95

Robert F. Calimeri (signature)

Forget the Novocaine, Doc— I was a Teacher

By

Robert F. Calimeri

Illustrations by

Scott J. Simolo

First published by AuthorHouse 04/16/04

ISBN: 1-4140-4676-6 (e-book)
ISBN: 1-4184-4165-1 (Paperback)
ISBN: 1-4184-4164-3 (Dust Jacket)

Library of Congress Control Number: 2003099933

This book is printed on acid free paper.

Printed in the United States of America
Bloomington, IN

CONTENTS

ACKNOWLEDGMENTS

I would like to thank the following people for reading the manuscript, or parts of it, and for making constructive comments, and sometimes other comments.

Jerry Calimeri	Patty Calimeri	Patsy Calimeri
Catherine Whittier	Ray Whittier	Rocco LoPiccolo
Jan LoPiccolo	Bill Huther	Carol Huther
Ted Davenport	Betty Davenport	Ethel Hughes
John Simolo	Mary Tucker	Olivia Cambs
Dottie Simolo	Paul Ferrari	Angela Daddabbo
Anne Fitzsimmons	Emily Fitzsimmons	Paul Guido
Jack Miller	Kaveh Shahidi	Rick Orser
Scott Simolo	David LoPiccolo	Mark LoPiccolo
Joy LoPiccolo	Amy McGhan	Ali Champagne
Judy Plis	Ken Plis	Susanne Fitzsimmons
Jack Palombella	Al Wilson	Finger Lakes Writers Group
Bill Tracy		
Tony LoCastro	Barbara LoCastro	Mike Clark
Sonny Marinelli	Marlene Marinelli	Bill Klink
Betty Klink	Louie Nocilly	Linda Riblet

Cover Photos

by

James P. Hughes

Thanks to my sister, Joanne, for being a wisecracker and to my brother, Claude, for encouraging her.

A special thanks to my wife, Barbara, for her encouragement.

A special thanks to Jim Hughes for his inimitable methods of making constructive criticisms.

A very special thanks to my brother, Jerome, for reading each revision and suggesting ways to make what was initially a brainstorming effort into something intelligible.

Thanks to anyone I left out.

DEDICATION

This book is dedicated, with love, to
my wife, Barbara, my children, Susan and Christopher,

and to the memory of

Billy and Coco

INTRODUCTION

I left the school building for the final time, late in the day, my old worn-out valise feeling heavy with the last of the personal possessions which had marked a few square feet of classroom space as my place in the scheme of things for the past thirty-three years. I had been anticipating this moment every day for the last two of them. At last I was a former teacher. But I felt neither joy nor relief, only emptiness and loneliness. Had my colleagues been right in saying that I would be lost outside the classroom? I drove around the parking lot one last time. And then again. And again. And again, until it was nearly dusk. Finally-mechanically-I headed for the highway.

Before I pulled onto the main road, I inspected my reflection in the sideview mirror. What was left of my hair was dull gray. My skin seemed wrinkled and spotted with age. There were dark, moist circles under my eyes, a rivulet upon my cheek.

As I drove home, I began thinking about the advice offered by my friends who had warned, "Bob, don't quit your day job."

I just did, I thought. Now what?

In fact, I still haven't really quit. But more on that later.

At home that evening I needed companionship, but I had nothing to say to anyone. My thoughts were jumbled and contradictory.

By the following morning, however, things were quite different. At breakfast, as I mulled over my three decades of public school teaching and coaching, the memories came flooding back. Oh sure, I had the occasional bouts with the administrative, guidance, clerical and maintenance staffs. But what teacher hasn't? There had been the give and take with fellow teachers and occasional testy competition among academic departments. And, of course, there were the many students—the true protagonists in the daily theatrical performances called American education. The students are the stars in their own little productions that play out in the halls and classrooms of your neighborhood public schools. In these ongoing shows you would find more drama, comedy, and tragedy than any theatergoer would find on the great stages of the world. And in the middle of an environment intended to foster hope, fun, and the love of learning, standing strong against the malaise and anxiety of academic and societal change, is the classroom teacher. And, proudly, I had been one. In my heart of hearts I suppose I shall always be one, but I just knew that it was the right time for me to go.

I got the bright idea that a lot of the stories I had gleaned from the classroom, the athletic field and life in general might be of interest to others. The "now what?" question has been answered. Here is *Forget the Novocaine, Doc— I was a Teacher*, a little tome the title of which was offered by my friend Jim Hughes and his wife, Ethel.

Most of what is written is true, but not all of it is intended to be taken seriously. Some of the names are fictitious, while the people they refer to are real, very real.

I hope that my forays into irony will be obvious.

"Just One More Time Around."

BOOK I

COLLEGE

1

MY GREAT EDUCATION

In 1963, freshly graduated from college and with a suitcase full of "worldly" experiences, I embarked on what I hoped would be a rewarding teaching career, armed with what I thought were impressive teaching credentials.

Sometimes the things we learn outside the classroom are at least as important as the things we learn inside it. The school of hard-knocks often provides invaluable and never forgotten lessons. I learned a great deal from that school.

Although my credentials were hard earned, I often wonder how some students ever become college graduates. To many youngsters, college is a time mainly for fun and frolic. My college fraternity friends and I spent a lot of time at a place called the "T," (which doesn't stand for library), located in the environs of the New York State College for Teachers, Albany, N.Y. This was our way of blowing off steam from the stresses and tedium of studying. We went "raging," as we called our barhopping, every weekend and usually got "blitzed," that is, everyone but me.

I was usually the designated driver because I had a penchant for picking the short straw. It never dawned on me until several years later that I had been "setup." I finally figured out why they always had me pick last.

I never knew which brother's rattletrap auto would be the vehicle of choice until a few minutes before departure time. Since the car usually had something malfunctioning, we kept our fingers crossed, hoping for a safe return after our fun evening.

One brother had a dual-exhaust clunker, and I always revved up the engine to see if I could break the sound barrier.

Since my limit was about two beers, I never got involved in the belching contests, those gross displays that are common on most campuses. The weekend ragers' goal was to spend the weekend convulsed in mirth and merriment. And they succeeded.

When I deposited the thoroughly sodden, bleary-eyed brothers into their respective rooms in our barely-livable frat house after their night of revelry, many of them appeared comatose, and the ones who weren't were clearly tottering as they entered their rooms muttering incoherently.

Actually, the hardest part was getting them to the second floor. On the way up, they always wanted to play a game called "slide down the banister." Their activities the next day usually included repairing their fun-slide, although they were rarely completely successful.

When I finally deposited then on their beds, they were soon kaput, dead to the world, carrying with them that stale stench of beer and cigarette smoke. Sweet dreams!

Occasionally during the night I would awaken to the sweet sounds of dry retching. Satisfied that all was right with the world, I would smile and drift back to sleep.

I never witnessed delirium tremens, although there were many hangovers the next day.

It must be noted that I too was a smoker. I was absolutely ecstatic, anticipating that first cigarette after pizza and beer. I often thought the beer makers, the pizza makers and the cigarette makers were in cahoots. I smoked for ten years, beginning in 1958, but more about that later.

Since none of us had the Midas touch, if the funds from home were late in arriving, we cronies journeyed to a little joint where the beers were a nickel a glass. Golly, I loved that cozy little taproom where the beer flowed freely and the chuckles and chortles were aplenty. Our thirst seemed unquenchable and it added to our boisterous fun. Every Monday was dubbed "aspirin day." Some of the social studies majors called it "hiatus day" as well. Most of them attached purloined "stop" signs to the doors of their rooms. They would do anything to get their rest.

Ah! We had the idyllic life, studying hard during the week but always looking forward to the indolent weekends. For those of us who had exams on Monday, Sunday was a day of lolling and improvisation, a little of this, a little of that, a little studying and lots of sleeping.

And always the certainty of a little mischief on those playful weekends. One time in a place called "The Arms," which wasn't a classy joint even by a long stretch of the imagination, but which met our needs very nicely, I was sitting observing the debauchery and jocularity around me when suddenly I noticed my roommate standing at the bar with his trousers around his ankles. The bartender with whom he was conversing was none-the-wiser. This ritual, "dropping trou" as it was called, could occur at any time and in any place.

That same night, another buddy was taken away in handcuffs. Apparently he had gotten into the hooch pretty well and was in a phone booth too long to suit one of the patrons. The guy kept pestering him to get out of the booth. He was a bit rowdy when he finally exited and rapped the patron in the forehead with the phone he had torn off the wall. The patron, an off-duty cop, wasn't too happy.

A ritual and specialty of one of the brothers was "heinie biting." Danny the mensch was the champion of this event, and no female heinie was exempt, be it patrician or plebeian, willowy or porcine, although he preferred one that was attached to a statuesque beauty that wasn't a bitch or a highbrow. Danny became very popular and the ladies felt like celebrities in his presence. When I asked him what was up with his behavior he said, "Cal, my peccadilloes are nothing more than a bit of benign debauchery, although it would be nice to be deflowered, too."

"Danny, that was the most eloquent circumlocution that I have ever heard you utter," I responded.

"Is that good or bad?" he inquired.

Danny was not one to rest on his laurels. Week after week he would indulge his chicanery. I felt like a voyeur when I was with him.

And on these rare occasions when Danny became lazy, Keith, his sidekick, would remind him of his legend—and once again he would become active.

Guys like me, who preferred their steak on a plate, were perceived as humdrum. We had to coax and wheedle in order to steal even a perfunctory kiss. My participation was limited to simply ogling the girls in hopes of getting their attention. Instead of giving me that come-hither look, their main reaction was usually, "What are you staring at?" The one time I did rouse a lady's smile, I tried to speak, froze, and simply stammered. Although my only goal was to do a little "canoodling," I always struck out. Such is the unpredictability of womankind.

Even when I tried a little flirty humor by inventing and uttering a clever double-entendre, it was futile and yet I had fun. Go figure!

Sometimes I wore my Charlie Chaplin chapeau and dapper duds. Although I looked quite natty in these fine threads, still no luck. The result was the same when I wore my folksy outfits.

My associates had their standards, however. Even they would not stoop to certain pranks.

One time, members of another fraternity lifted part of a bull's anatomy from a meat-processing house, thank goodness, and "hung" it from a window in the women's dorm. Brothers from my fraternity thought the prank was in poor taste. Their breasts swelled with pride and self-righteousness as they condemned an act that was beneath them.

Some of the habits and superstitions that undergraduates develop on campus are really bizarre. My erstwhile roommate never changed his clothes or shaved during exam week. One time somebody wanted to give him money because the Samaritan thought he was a homeless panhandler. This is the same guy who would study for exams with two quarts of beer in tow. He said it quenched his thirst, while helping him to think and remember. I guess social studies majors can do that.

As a math and science major, I thought of myself on a higher plane, so my feelings were recently hurt when my former colleague, Linda, who had been at Albany when I was there, said that the primary objective of the members of my college fraternity was to "nail" every co-ed on campus. I took exception to the word "nail."

We were living the life of Riley, and we knew it.

As a reminder of those life-of-Riley days, when I left Albany for the last time, I took with me an aesthetically pleasing tankard, embossed with "Albany State" and "Cal," from which I still drink an occasional brew for old times' sake.

So there were two parts to my education, the academic part and the very social part. Having the proper mix of both prepared me for a very successful teaching career, if you ask me.

"Wasn't That Fun?"

2

MY ROOMMATES

Fate had brought me to these happy circumstances through slow, painful steps. During the fall of 1960, after graduating from Auburn Community College (ACC) and transferring to Albany, I lived in a rooming house on Cortland Place. Since it was a lonely existence, I moved into a dorm for the spring semester. My roommate was a guy that everybody called "Ace." Through Ace's persuasion, I later joined the fraternity, whose goals, I thought, were academic.

It was during the academic year 1961-1962 that things got really "crazy." The fraternity house I lived in on Washington Ave. was conveniently located right across from the "T." The prevalent opinion was that we were an "animal house," but the reality was that we were merely boys having fun.

The following year, I shared a small upstairs apartment with three frat brothers, "The Naz," "The Wiz," and "Ace." There was to be a division of labor, each brother taking a turn cooking. However, after I flubbed-up my first assignment by making burned hamburgers that were the size of half-dollars, I was demoted to permanent dishwasher.

On weekends we would go "stomping," as The Naz called our outings for fun and merriment. Stomping was a step below raging and was testimony to our growing maturity.

Sometimes two townies, Joe and Willie, would be our companions for the evening. Willie was a very generous man—on more than one occasion he paid me $20 for a Saturday's worth of manual labor for his construction company. Of course I blew the $20 that evening for food and libation.

Joe and his brother, Lee, owned a restaurant where we went many times for breakfast, sometimes very early in the morning. I recently saw Joe for the first time in thirty years. He is exactly the same, although a little paunchy. With his staccato speech and mannerisms, I thought I was in the presence of the actor, Joe Pesci.

During my final semester at school, my roommates were two fraternity brothers, Dick and Peter, and our apartment was on Western Ave. It wasn't much, but it was ours. One brother was straight-laced while the other had some peculiar tendencies. His cooking was *par excellence* and his spaghetti sauce was the best. When I asked him why he always made sauce while in the nude, he said, "I feel very free and my creative juices seem to flow more easily."

"The real reason is clearly visible to me; I think you're just bragging," I responded.

One time we got a call from Dick's mother, Mary. She and Dick's sister, Maria, were preparing to drive from Syracuse to Albany to visit Dick. While they were en route, Dick insisted that we clean up our messy apartment in order to impress his mom. We worked feverishly for three hours, checking every nook and cranny, capering here, there, and everywhere until the place was spotless and my whiskbroom was worn out.

Among other things, the week-old spaghetti dishes were finally washed, the many empty beer bottles that cluttered the pad were disposed of, and the clothes that had been strewn about were neatly folded and put away. We congratulated each other on a job well done.

When they arrived, Mary said, "What a pigpen! This place is filthy!" On a positive note, she didn't call it a cesspool. We never told her we had cleaned for three hours.

One of my favorite times in that apartment occurred when I was in solitude. I would sit in an old, comfortable, threadbare sofa with my bag of Oreo cookies, a banana and a glass of milk. While eating, I would also be singing a tune from a popular TV ad. That famous ditty, "Little girls have pretty curls, but I like Oreos," was like a mantra for me. I'm embarrassed to say that I never shared my Oreos with anyone.

Our pad was a haven for moochers who frequently crashed there on weekends. One guy, Duke, whose favorite saying was, "Woe is me, Cal! Can I crash here awhile?" often prepared baloney sandwiches...at two A.M....with our baloney, of course. Occasionally he brought hors d'oeurves, usually consisting of saltine crackers and nothing more. Big deal!

Food was always of paramount importance to us growing boys. During one exam week, famished from studying all day, my roommates and I traveled to a little restaurant called "The Moon" five nights in a row at 11 P.M., for macaroni. Of course, we always got a side order of delicious meatballs. As a treat, we washed everything down with a little libation. For me, it was like an unction, so soothing that it enabled me to sleep like a baby.

Whether money was tight or not (it usually was), apartment mooching was common. There was always someone who was willing to take you in for whatever rent you could afford, even if it was zero. Strangers often depended on our bounty as well.

One summer I crashed with my pal Tony (he preferred the nickname "Osh," so that's what we called him).

The night before we moved into Osh's summer residence, he and I stayed in the men's on-campus dormitory.

This turned out to be a strange land, indeed. I thought I was going to lose my mind. There was no furniture in the room to absorb sound, except for two beds. As Osh slept, he alternately snorted and wheezed in an endless cacophony from hell.

He continued with these most god-awful noises all night long, the sounds reverberating from wall to wall. It was the kind of torture that you hear about during wartime. Fortunately for me, I snored as loudly as he did, so I could give him back some of his own medicine. Sure enough, the next morning Osh complained about my snoring. I said, "That's a joke, right?" He just laughed. I didn't tell him that he got the best of me. I just wallowed in self-pity or bumped into things like a zombie for most of the day.

"Osh, does snoring run in your family as it does in mine?" I asked as we drove to the summer apartment.

"Cal, only my older brother Tony snores."

"Your older brother who?" I asked.

"You heard me right, and I don't want to talk about it."

Ordinarily Osh is imperturbable and outwardly languid. In fact there were times when I thought he was sleepwalking. Since I had obviously struck a nerve, I dropped the subject.

Several years later I was having a conversation with Osh's sister, Loretta, so I inquired about her two brothers named Tony. She said, "Bob, it would be better if you were to 'furgeddaboudit.'"

"O.K.," I weakly responded.

During that same summer in Albany, Dick and a friend named Mike lived with Osh and me for several weeks.

As though trying to prove that they weren't the sharpest knives in the drawer, Dick and Mike went hunting and brilliantly left their dog, a beautiful Weimaraner, locked in a company car.

When they returned after two hours, the car interior was in shambles. Everything was torn apart, even the dashboard. The hubbub that ensued was about which of them was the stupidest. They decided to call it a draw by admitting that they were both quite obtuse.

Then the geniuses took a hammer to the car's exterior, staging vandalism. "Dog, huh?" said the body shop owner, when they took it in for repairs.

I can only imagine what the insurance adjuster said.

Osh confronted Dick and Mike and said, "I guess you guys refuse to display even a tincture of cerebral activity."

Their only response was "What?"

Finely, after 38 years of marriage, I went to a sleep clinic in 2001 to get help with my snoring problem. The diagnostic report said, "Eight awakenings and 231 arousals." I was proud that age hadn't diminished my virility.

The other day Osh and Dick were in town, so I had them over for a few brews and stuffed peppers by the pool. One thing led to another and, to certify my virility, I gave them the diagnostic report to read. Osh read the report out loud, and he and Dick burst out laughing when he read the footnote that I had overlooked. *Arousal*, it said was "any change in body position."

Of all the characters I roomed with during my college days, my buddy, Peter, was the closest to me. He and I had some especially great times together. On several occasions at a joint called "The Hen," we would burst into spontaneous song, usually singing "Unchained Melody" or "You'll Never Walk Alone." We were into karaoke before it became really popular.

The bartender didn't care for us, probably because he thought we were bellowing and we thought we were crooning.

One time he called the cops. I didn't believe that he had made the call because I could have sworn that his finger was holding down the lever on the receiver. I told him he was bluffing, but when the cops arrived he said, "That's him," as he pointed at me. Since I was the only one taken outside in handcuffs, I figured that Peter had become invisible. When the officers put me into the paddy wagon, I started to sweat because I imagined all the horrible things that could happen to me, not to mention the headlines in the Auburn paper: "Hometown College Boy Thrown into Hoosegow."

Fortunately there was a happy ending. Peter finally showed up and used his considerable charm to convince the officers to remove the shackles and release me. I'm not sure what he told them, but as we walked away from the cops, he whispered to me to hunch my shoulders and shuffle my feet as though I were slow witted. When we were safely around the corner, we burst into song: "When you walk through a storm…" and continued singing all the way home.

At the end of that academic year as we were departing for our respective homes, I asked Peter, "Why do I feel as though I passed college but I'm flunking life?"

His only response was, "Me too, Cal, me too."

BOOK II
PERSONALS

3

WHY THERAPY

My days as a softball pitcher may have contributed to my need for therapy. I became "shell-shocked" during those days, because subsequent to delivering my pitch, which some described as seeing a watermelon coming in, I frequently had to duck the batted ball as it buzzed my head. At least I gave my teammates ample opportunity to display their defensive skills. After we lost the first three games, I was certain we would win the next one; then I was certain we would win the next one.... Oh, how my teammates suffered! They welcomed the brief moments of repose between innings. Finally I got the message and retired after that 0-10 season.

To add insult to injury, there were two pitchers who were not nice to me. Dudley Deadly would often warn batters before intentionally hitting them. After releasing his 90 mph fastball, he would yell, "look out," a phrase that was useless to me. If he got two strikes on me, he would yell, "sit down" on the next pitch, and I did. Dudley's favorite form of exercise now is walking his little dog, Bridget.

Big Daddy was a different story. He said he never intentionally hit me, but he was so wild that I was usually trembling whenever I faced him. I just saw him the other day, and this 330-pounder had me feel his still huge biceps. By coincidence, Big Daddy's favorite exercise is also walking his little dog, Morgan.

As for me, I don't have a dog.

Although Dudley and Big Daddy learned to pitch by aping New York State Softball Hall Of Fame pitcher "Monk" Curtin, there was one major difference between Monk and everybody else. Monk would usually *strike out* the batter. Rarely, if ever, would he *strike the batter*!

I was pretty shaken, embarrassed, and depressed after the season. It was hard to make eye contact with my teammates whenever I saw them around town.

Although I considered and rejected the need for therapy, its desirability was resurrected as my teaching career progressed.

"Sit Down!"

4

WITH A LITTLE HELP FROM
MODERN SCIENCE

Therapy definitely may be needed after a crisis as a way to get back on track. I never failed to convey that concept to my students when I noticed that they were having tough times, especially emotionally. "Talk to someone, but certainly not me," I urged them.

Although I was involved in teaching for thirty-three years (thirteen in biology and twenty in mathematics), I enjoyed all but thirty of those years.

During the other three years I was undergoing intensive psychotherapy to repair the damage. The psychotherapy lasted three years before I was permanently cured the first time.

The second time I was permanently cured was after the 1988 cross-country season. I was the coach of the girls' team. That time it took only one year to cure me, and I'll proudly show my "Permanently Cured" papers to anyone who doubts me.

I'm learning to play the guitar as part of my ongoing therapy. I wrote a song entitled "I Took the Cure." I sing it to the tune of "On Top of Old Smoky."

In addition to the psychotherapy and the music therapy, modern science may play a role in my quest for total recovery. Scientists, mapping the entire genome, have learned a great deal about chromosome 22.

Now the key for me is that it is believed that the genes on chromosome 22 play an important role in mental health. I have been told many times by friends, relatives, and colleagues that good "mental health" should be a primary goal of mine, mainly because I often display my copious oddment arsenal. So, hopefully within my lifetime doctors can send a benign vector, carrying a normal gene, to the proper locus of my chromosome 22, and I won't have to get a third set of papers because my DNA program glitch will finally be corrected.

This breakthrough in genetics may be a double-edged sword, however, because while insidious diseases may become extinct, abuses of "cloning" may become prevalent.

The quest for "designer humans" may come into vogue. Put your order in for Liz Taylor eyes, blond hair, tall and muscular, high I.Q., et cetera. Won't that be wonderful! We may be able to design our own children or make everyone look alike, thus eliminating problems associated with race and ethnicity. Don't be surprised if some day while you are out on a leisurely stroll, you see yourself walking down the opposite side of the street.

Picture this. You are at Fenway Park in Boston and the announcer gives the Red Sox lineup: "Batting 1st and playing 1st base, Ted Williams One; batting 2nd and playing 2nd base, Ted Williams Two...batting 8th and catching, Ted Williams Eight and batting 9th and pitching, Pedro Martinez One." Won't that be grand?

And we owe the beginning of all this to the Austrian monk, Gregor Mendel, and his experiments with garden peas.

Who would have dreamed that his experiments with lowly garden peas might some day lead to a bunch of clones running around a baseball field?

Personally, I'd rather not see that happen. It's good enough for me that God created sex, and that's that.

Natural processes have worked quite well in producing little clones. After I had been in the classroom for what seemed like forever, I began to see the second generation of many of my students. It was surrealistic to interact with these little natural clones. I often saw them "walk the walk, and talk the talk" of their parents. "Hey, you taught my father" or "you taught my mother," they would say. I retired before they had a chance to say, "Hey, you taught my grandfather or grandmother."

As Yogi Berra might say, "It was *déjà vu* all over again."

"You've Got To Be Kidding!"

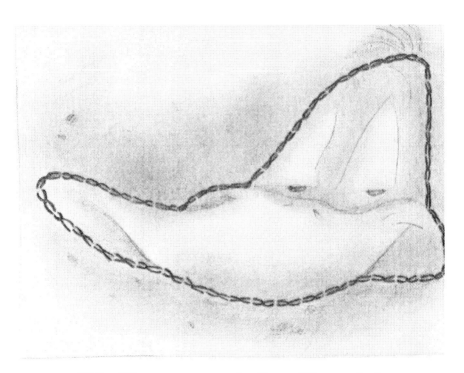

"My Chromosomes As Seen Through A Microscope in 1972."

"Oh, I Took The Cure…"

5

SLOW ON THE UPTAKE

Although I respond quite well to surprises, there is evidence that points to a gap in my comprehension of certain things—like the time I was learning to play bridge, a complicated card game. During lunch one day I was asked to fill in as a fourth. "Sure, I have never played the game," I said, "but if it's anything like Pinochle, I might be mildly competent."

"You'll do," they said.

They gave me a crash course in bidding and the game started. While I like to try new games, occasionally I don't catch on very quickly. I was told that you needed 13 points to open. I was the first bidder, and I passed because I didn't have the required number of points. Everybody else passed as well. When we showed our hands, my partner nearly jumped over the table to get at me. "You fool, you have twenty-five high card points," he cried. "Why did you pass?"

Being the good math teacher that I was, I said, "You didn't tell me I needed *at least* thirteen points to open; I thought you meant *precisely* 13 points." People should say what they mean. I have heard that marriages have broken up over this game. I can see why.

There was another time when something didn't dawn on me right away. I was filling in as a long-term sub for a biology instructor, and I asked a question to which one student gave a beautiful explanation. The next day, the topic came up again and I asked her to explain again. She responded with: "I really don't understand the material."

Boy, was I confused. I said, "That's impossible; how can you forget completely overnight?" The bell rang before I got an answer. After school the girl visited my classroom. Five seconds later her sister, with obvious identical DNA, walked in. I knew I had been had as I blushed to a beautiful crimson. I was the only one fooled by their little switcheroo. The next day the class got a good laugh out of that one.

One time I stopped at a gas station to get gas for my snowblower. I pulled up to the pump and retrieved the gas can from the back seat. As I drove away after getting a gallon of gas, I noticed that the light on the dashboard was on, signaling that one of my car doors was not completely closed. I stopped, got out of the car, and closed the back door on the driver's side. When I got back into the car I noticed that the panel light was still on. So, I got out of the car again and checked all the doors. They were all properly closed, but the light was still on. After I checked the doors for the third time, it finally dawned on me that the indicator light was on because the door I was getting in and out of was always open. I finally did figure it out. That's the important thing, and it made me feel good.

"Oh, Now I Get It!"

6

PARALYSIS BY ANALYSIS

We had an outstanding bowler at Tyburn Academy, a small, private school where I have been teaching part-time since my retirement. Francis recently had an amazing 770-series in a national tournament. So, he was eminently qualified to hear my story and make a suggestion or two.

Before the advent of automatic pin-setting machines, I was a member of a pin-boy league that competed every Saturday at the Polish Falcons on Pulaski Street, in Auburn. I remember carrying my bowling ball, in the dead of winter, as I walked the one-mile to the lanes and the one-mile back home. "Can you imagine asking a fourteen or fifteen year old to do that today, Francis?" I said.

"The response would be interesting," he muttered.

I told him that every time I go by the Owasco Outlet, which is on that one-mile route from long ago, I look into the water to see if I can locate my bowling ball. Since my bowling average had flattened out, never to rise above 161, no matter how hard I tried, I decided that the little fishes could use my ball as part of their biological niches. It is still there, after forty years, only now it is a haven for the little creatures.

"It's awful when one's mind gets in the way of simple things, isn't it Mr. Cal?" Francis said. "You recall the saying about 'paralysis by analysis,' don't you?"

"I have heard of it, but I have never experienced it," I said.

He told me that finding the balance in life is the key to health and happiness. Not doing things to excess is the way to get there: don't overeat; don't overwork; don't overstudy; don't overexercise; and whatever you do, don't overanalyze. Moderation is the mantra. I pondered this and wondered how such a young man had become so wise.

"Maybe you should take up bowling again, since you have been permanently cured," he said.

"How did you know that?" I inquired.

"You told us, remember?"

"Of course I remember; I was just testing you."

The wise young man told me that maybe I had been thinking too much or maybe I was releasing the ball incorrectly, and he would give me a lesson or two. And, he did.

I haven't taken up bowling again, yet, but I'm reading lots of books and magazines about bowling and I am watching the pros on television and I am practicing a shadow-release of the ball, with my glove on. I have determined the volume and color of the ideal ball and I used geometry to determine the optimum placement of the finger holes. When I have everything worked out, I will buy a new, perfect ball and begin practicing for a year or two before I join a league. My goal will be to average at least 162.

7

LOOK, I'M SKIING

In February, 2002, during a typical Central New York winter, fifteen teen-agers and five adults from Tyburn Academy traveled to idyllic Loon Mountain, located in Lincoln, New Hampshire for two days of skiing.

For me, the virgin skier, it was a disaster as well as a highlight of my life. On the one hand, I spent most of the time sprawled on my back. On the other hand, in a perverse and masochistic way, it felt good and I had loads of fun.

When we arrived at our A-frame lodge, a member of our group, a delicate and not-used-to-roughing-it adult wouldn't step inside for fear of catching something nasty or seeing little critters skittering around. When the rest of us marched into the cabin without hesitation, the dainty one had no choice but to follow. Needless to say, Janet had a ball.

That first evening, Wednesday, we rested, ate a hearty meal, sang, and played games.

Then it was time for bed. The girls slept upstairs, the boys downstairs, and I was exiled to the couch because of my snoring.

Thursday morning, bright and early we headed for the slopes, some 45 minutes away. Upon arrival, I was immediately in awe of the natural charm and picturesque beauty of the landscape. Soon I would be part of it.

After I was outfitted with short skis for beginners, and while most of the group headed for the mountain, five of us took a lesson.

If I agreed to raise her math grade five points, one of the girls, Amy, agreed to help me up each time I fell. While the teen-agers zipped right through each exercise, I stumbled awkwardly, sliding every which way, inevitably landing on my rear end. When the lesson was over, I knew that I had received the better of the deal; a tired Amy agreed. Little did I know at the time that my gyrations were a portent of great challenges that lay ahead.

After the lesson, while the others headed for the slopes, I headed for the flat area in back of the lodge. This gave me an opportunity to limber up my rickety old legs. Soon I had mastered the "flats," so my friend Kevin and I headed for the lift that was to take us to the top of the "Bunny" slope. Incidentally, there is no way that hill can be called a "Bunny" slope in New York State. It was more like a "Jackrabbit" slope, and that's what I dubbed it.

I had been warned repeatedly to be careful when getting off the lift. Several experienced skiers, and our host, Todd, who was the coach of the MIT ski team, had told me of the perils of moments of inattention to that tricky maneuver.

Sure enough their direst concerns came to pass. As I left the seat of the lift, I became disoriented while trying to maintain my balance, careened left down a little slope, fell on my rear end, and banged the back of my head on the snow. I am thankful that the snow was soft, but I assure you it left an impression on me, not to mention the embarrassment I felt.

When my friends came to rescue me, I told them that I had an irresistible impulse to make a snow angel. I don't think they believed me.

Then, the real trial began. I tried to snowplow; I tried to go across the slope; I tried everything that the experts told me to do. Everything failed. Fortunately for me, Kevin is a strong guy. He said, "Bob, I have an idea; I am going to ski you down the mountain." With his hands on my shoulders, he literally skied slowly backward down the mountain, supporting all 200 pounds of me. I fell several times and knocked him down once. Kevin is young and strong and a good skier, but navigating me to the bottom of the hill nearly did him in. When the end was in sight, my guess is that Kevin had also aged several more years.

Finally at the bottom, Kevin was completely exhausted. Gasping for air, he weakly said, "I would prefer not to see you again until tomorrow," and then he disappeared.

Although I was baffled by his comment I experienced an exhausting exhilaration, but I kept a low profile for the rest of the morning.

After lunch, Michael and Jennifer convinced me that they had found an easy slope to the left of the Jackrabbit, and up we went. I did better than I had on the first run, but still fell a lot. At my age, it was hell trying to get up. Most of the time in order to become upright again, I took one ski off. This worked quite well, but it was slow going. Stimulated by the encouragement of my two student companions, I resolved that I would "ski."

Suddenly, I was in determination mode and totally focused. Off I went. I made the mistake of the novice by getting my skis parallel and pointed down the mountain. I flew for about 40 meters. I remember saying to myself, "I'm skiing; I'm Billy Kidd." And then the reality of the moment dawned on me. "I need to stop before I die."

I recalled the instructor saying, "When all else fails, sit down." Since I was in runaway mode, I did just that and went "buttock over teakettle."

Michael and Jennifer appeared out of nowhere and said, "Mr. Cal, you were really skiing. You were flying!" They followed this praise with a sudden paroxysm of laughter.

"Did you try to kill me?" I responded as I rubbed my elbow and laughed at the same time. They laughed even louder as they skied away.

Needless to say, I was the topic of conversation for the next several days. I felt so proud. I take victories wherever I can find them.

On Friday, my colleague Ann insisted that I try again. Like Kevin, Ann is a seasoned veteran skier, so I consented to place my life in her hands and through her patience and encouragement, I slowly descended the mountain.

Although I fell several times and was weary at the bottom, I felt good because I was in one piece. I thought I'd had a better run than the first two, so I was surprised when Ann told everyone that I was her greatest challenge. "Just kidding, Bob," she told me later.

Fortunately our pleasurable jaunt was almost over, because after Kevin, Michael, Jennifer and Ann, I was running out of skiing companions.

All in all, I had a great time. Even the indoor activities, singing, playing cards and charades, were fun.

We feasted on baked macaroni, baked chicken, and on the hit of the trip, the big pot of chili made by my wife, Barbara.

I brought back a perpetual reminder of this fabulous adventure, the crooked and still painful pinky on my left hand. But it's a good pain in the same sense as a good exhaustion after a day of working outdoors.

I got my crooked pinky conquering the mountain, and I raised that pinky proudly.

"I've Got You Big Guy!"

Fun On The Jackrabbit.

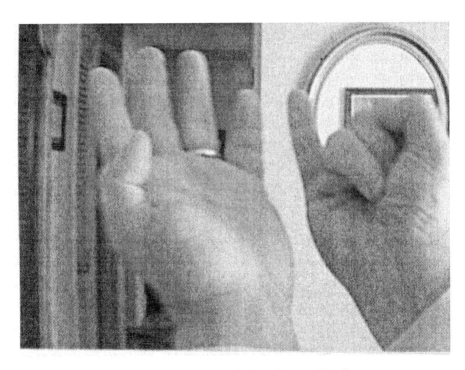

"I Raised My Pinky Proudly."

8

FEAR

There was one time during my coaching days when fear dominated my thoughts.

One spring, my track team was to compete in the Baldwinsville Invitational. The arthritis in my knee was flaring up, so I put an external cast over my pants and the team and I proceeded on our merry way to the meet.

On the return trip, the pain in my leg was almost unbearable. When we arrived back at school, I could not lift my leg to get into my car. I hobbled to the phone, which fortunately was located in front of the school building. No one answered at my home. As luck would have it, I remembered the phone number of my friend Tony who lived nearby. Tony came right up and hassled me about my apparent inability to take care of myself. I was in too much pain to argue with him. Besides, maybe he was right. He took me home, but it became obvious that I needed to go to the emergency room. Tony consented to take me and stayed with me throughout the entire experience.

Fate delivered me into the hands of a very young ER doctor who insisted on "tapping" my swollen knee in order to give me relief. As I lay on the gurney, the doctor appeared with a very large syringe. Although I was sweating and a bit frightened, the thought of relief dominated my thinking. Into the knee joint went the needle. When he pulled back on the plunger, he got no fluid. So he proceeded to move the needle around, hoping to find the right spot. Still no fluid. I almost passed out because of the pain. Still no fluid. He finally removed the needle from my knee.

"I want to try one more time," he said confidently.

"Doc," I begged, "please, no more. I can't take it again."

"Keep a stiff upper lid, lad," he said as he jabbed me again before I could escape.

When the second penetration didn't work, he did it a third time before I could protest. As he moved the needle around in the joint, I could envision its point tearing my knee to shreds. Tears filled my eyes.

Finally, he withdrew the needle again without fluid and apologized for the "unavoidable" pain he had caused me.

Terror struck, I stumbled away as fast as possible. Tony was right behind me.

Through all of my agony, Tony had been laughing a deep, sinister belly laugh. And still he laughed. And laughed. And laughed 'til he could laugh no more. I have known Tony all my life, and in the last forty years, I have heard him laugh just four times, including the deep belly laugh he was exhibiting on that memorable day. At the time, I failed to appreciate what was so funny, but from the perspective of many years, I realize that he must have needed that emotional release very much. I'm glad that I was able to help him out.

The next day I went to a sports medicine doctor, a real doctor, in Syracuse to get relief. While the doctor successfully tapped my knee on the first try, I told him the story about my anguish with the ER doctor. When he began to laugh, I asked him if he was related to Tony. He laughed even louder.

As I drove home from the doctor's office, I was ecstatic with relief. Since my thinking was now more lucid, I decided to bide my time until the opportune moment presented itself to deal with Tony.

That moment did appear a few years later, and it was an exhilarating experience. One day my friends, Sonny, Tony, and I and our respective wives were coming back home from beautiful Saratoga where we made our annual "donation" to the coffers of New York State while playing the ponies at the flat track. Sonny was driving and Tony was riding shotgun.

Shotgun Tony soon fell asleep and I saw my chance. In a moment of inspiration, I was able to inveigle a sanitary napkin from one of the women. I proceeded to tape the pad to Tony's bald head, or more correctly to the twenty-three-foot-long strand of hair he weaved back and forth across the top of his head. Sonny saw what I was doing and said, "Bo, you are really sick." I replied that that was a given and was the reason why I was licensed to do what I was doing. While Tony slept, we all enjoyed the joke, even Sonny and his wife, Marlene, who laughed hysterically and wet her pants. When Tony heard the commotion and realized what I had done, he became enraged and embarrassed. I knew exactly how he felt.

I still remember his glee at my suffering in the emergency room.

When I told that story to my sister, Joanne, she said, "You know, Bo, sometimes I think you suffer from cranial-rectal inversion."

"What," I said.

"Think about it," she said, "but make sure you're standing up so you can breathe."

"I don't get it," I said.

She just smiled.

Sometimes it takes me an extended period of time to get over things. One time Tony and I were golfing at a beautiful course in Myrtle Beach. We had paired up with two locals and were having a grand time. Tony was very impressive, and the one female in the foursome kept encouraging him with compliments. After ten holes Tony was five under par, and I said out of the blue, "Tony, you are playing so well that I forgive you for what you did to me in the ER room, and by the way, you are on your way to breaking the course record." That's all it took. He ended up shooting one over par.

I had not meant to jinx Tony, but I did enjoy the result.

Regardless of any latent sadistic tendencies that Tony has, he and his wife, Barbara, are wonderful people. One time Barbara let me borrow a dollar for something, under the condition that I would pay her back the next day.

"Which Knee Was That?"

"Revenge Is Sweet!"

9

A DAY AT THE RACES

We may have to rethink our annual trek to Saratoga, especially after what happened on August 2-4, 2002.

Friday, on the thruway, a motorist threw my brother-in-law the "bird" for cutting him off. To this day Bill denies that he cut the guy off.

Then, to add insult to injury the motorist yelled, "You're old so it doesn't matter if you die, but I'm young and I want to live."

Also on Friday I threw away my only winner for the day, a ninth race "exacta." Since we planned to leave the track before the eighth race, and check the results at home, I placed bets on the eighth race and the ninth race at the same time. Unfortunately for me, we decided to stay for the eighth race. I had no winners so I threw away all the tickets in my pocket, totally forgetting about my ninth race exacta bet.

While watching the ninth race at our vacation residence, I realized what I had done. When the exacta came in and paid $95, I felt sick. Ten years ago I would have had a fit of rage, but because of my new found maturity, I wallowed in self-pity awhile but soon returned to my normal self, after a good cry.

When we returned to the track on Saturday, I asked an attendant if he had seen my ticket. While he looked at me kind of funny, my companions choked with laughter, and to this day they haven't let me live it down.

Not everything went wrong that weekend, however, since my friend Dudley saved the day by getting Hall of Fame jockey Jerry Bailey's autograph at a restaurant.

Unbeknownst to me, Dudley quickly crafted a plan to get the autograph. As Bailey and his family were preparing to leave their table after dinner, Dudley left our table and rushed into the bar. When Bailey got to three little stairs that led to the bar, he had to slow his pace. Precisely at that moment Dudley, now coming in the opposite direction, met the jockey. "Hey, nice race in the feature today," said Dudley.

"Thanks, I wish all my races were that easy," said Bailey.

Then Dudley presented Bailey with a small piece of yellow paper and asked for an autograph—he got it.

I have to admit that Dudley's plan was ingenious. I wish I had thought of it.

When Dudley returned to our table he had a big grin on his face. "I will treasure this," he said, as he showed us the autograph.

"You are remarkable," said Dudley's wife, Lou.

The other day I asked him if he had framed the autograph. Looking forlorn, he replied, "I can't find it."

10

GOOD SPORT

My wife has been a good sport about most of my adventures. For example, one night she allowed me to drag her out into a dark, murky swamp for a ride on an airboat.

I had been working at the Montezuma National Wildlife Refuge, near Auburn, in the summer of 1972, and I asked her to go out with me to "bun hole" ducks, a term used for determining their gender. I don't know how I talked her into it, because she often found it very stressful to do things with me.

Barbara sat on one side of the airboat, with me on the other and off we went into the darkness. The blackness of the night and a full moon gave an eerie quality, as though danger was lurking. However, we forged ahead.

It really is a skill catching the elusive mallards, wood ducks, et cetera with a net attached to a long pole. It can also be dangerous, especially if the net gets stuck in the mud. Well, we persevered, and she had the time of her life.

She netted several ducks and it was hilarious watching her trying to get them from the net into the storage box.

On the way home from the refuge, we made a pact to try to do more fun things together. I reminded her of the cliché, "Youth is wasted on the young," and continued with "but that's not going to happen to us." "Remember," I said, "when you are young, you really don't know what old is. Only after you are old can you know what young is."

Barbara just looked at me silently.

The next day the airboat sank while it was out on another mission.

Barbara maintains to this very moment, some thirty years later, that she did not enjoy the adventure. But, I know that in her heart of hearts, she really did.

My friends think my wife is a saint.

"I'll Get Them."

11

OH, DIRECTOR

The most benign things can be hazardous to one's health.

I recently had a bit part in a play, written and directed by my friend Ted. During one scene and costume change, the female lead, a heavenly buxom and voluptuous lady, turned quickly and hit me in the head with her ample bosom. I said, "If you do that three more times, I'm going to tell the director." I did, too.

During that play, I also learned something about myself. The adult playing the teen-age lead was supposed to slap her father in one scene. She kept wimping-out in rehearsal. Finally, in frustration, I resorted to a desperate move. I stood directly in front of her and said, "Slap me, bitch." That provided the necessary motivation. On the fourth take, with fire in her eyes, she let me have it from both sides.

"Good," I said, "now you've got it."

The thing I learned is that I liked it.

Through that experience I realized that since I didn't have the talent to be an athlete, maybe I could be an actor…or a professional masochist.

12

A DAY AT THE OCEAN

Because we were afflicted with insatiable wanderlust, Barbara and I and my in-laws, Betty and Bill usually traveled every spring to some far-away place. Thus, we creatively dubbed ourselves the "Farkels," because we traveled *far* and wide. Florida, Aruba (once), and California were frequent destinations.

On a trip to San Diego, one of my objectives was to bring back some small Pacific Ocean rocks for an earth science class that was being taught by a friend of mine.

While we were hiking along the many rocks, which lined the shore, I spied a smooth, pure white beauty of a small rock, but I didn't take it because a sign on the beach said, "Don't Take Anything From The Ocean."

After hiking three-quarters of a mile, we discovered a cave at the base of a cliff. We decided to explore it. Bill and I decided that the girls should go in first. They did. After we determined that it was safe, Bill and I went in also. Bill was so excited that he dropped his pants as an act of celebration. Forever more, that cave will be known to the Farkels as "Moon Cave" to commemorate Bill's moon.

On the way back from the cave, I fell behind the rest of the group, because my legs really hurt, especially my thighs, and I wasn't in very good shape anyway. Then, I got a bright idea. I started to limp. When the rest of the group turned around to check on me, they saw me limping and waited till I caught up. They said, "Did you hurt yourself?"

"No", I said, "I was just practicing in case I really got hurt." The only laughter I heard was my own.

I said I was sorry, but no one spoke another word to me until we got back to our room.

"Betty, Will You Go In First?"

BOOK III

HIGH SCHOOL DAYS

13

ISN'T FOOTBALL SEASON OVER YET?

On my drive home from college, after graduation, I began to anticipate the successful teaching career that would surely lie head. I imagined that my future would be filled with peace and tranquility.

In 1963, a person with teaching certification usually had his pick of jobs, especially if his credentials were in math or science. I was offered three jobs in three days, including one at my alma mater, which I ultimately selected. So, I packed my brand new valise with essential tools and off I went to save the world as a brand new biology teacher.

I wondered whether I would be a successful teacher like C. L. or would I be more like Stan, both of whom were favorite role models for me. But more on Stan later.

C. L. Willie taught history and social studies. I always smiled when I thought about my days as a student in his class. Every week or so he would calculate student grades and seat students accordingly. The students with the best grades for the week were assigned seats in the back of the room. Those with the worst grades were assigned to the front.

During football season of my senior year, I was assigned a seat in the front. I reasoned that I was always too tired to study, and thus my location was preordained.

One day C.L. asked, "Bob, when are you going to move to the back of the room?"

I responded with, "As soon as football season is over."

"Great, I'll remember that," he said.

I realized later that I had given C.L. ammunition to display his great wit, which was usually accompanied by great irony.

One day in early May, C.L. walked to my desk in the front of the room with his face showing its perpetual grin, looked me right in the eye and asked, "Bob, isn't football season over with yet?"

Perplexed, I said, "Of course. It ended in November." The class burst out in laughter, while I was pondering the essence of his question. It had to be explained to me by a friend before I came to the realization that I *really did belong* in the front of the room.

While C.L.'s classes were always lively, he actually saved me from a lot of mental stress. One day he said, "Bob, you'll never grow up to be called 'Mr. President.'" The pressure was now off, so I stopped trying. For that insight, I thank him.

I must also give him credit for my decision, from the first day of my teaching career until the last, to always locate my desk in the back of the room, never the front.

14

THAT WINNING SEASON

In addition to football, I participated in track and field during my high school days. I was a decent sprinter and an average long-jumper.

What are the chances that four "sixtysomethings," who were teammates many long years ago, are still alive and living in their hometown?

Well, after forty-five years, that is exactly the case for the members of the 1957 Auburn High School 880-yard relay team. It was a team that won the Section III championship, set a new Section III record, and placed fourth at the New York State meet held at West Point.

Although we have all gone our separate ways, we occasionally bump into each other around town and give a wave, or briefly reminisce about our glory days, as aging former athletes tend to do.

From time to time I still pull out the old black-and-white photographs of the crew and marvel at the slim, trim, and well-muscled physiques of the youths staring back at me. Ah, where did the years go?

The names of the guys are probably familiar to many around Auburn. In that great year of 1957, a typical race went something like this:

William "Butch," with his hackles up, leads off and gets a slight lead.

Bob "Bo" gets the handoff and promptly loses the lead.

Fred "Chuckles" regains the lead and extends it.

Tom "Mercury," our anchor, motors in for the win. "I never coasted in my life," says Tom.

Coach Blatz was an expert at assigning a relay order that would produce the optimum result. You can easily see why Chuckles was my favorite teammate.

It should be noted that Tom could run a 10.0 flat 100 yards, an excellent time for those days, and on cinders no less. This would translate into about a 9.8 on today's all-weather tracks. Every time I think about those old tracks, I am reminded of the pain in my feet from too-tight shoes and the burning shin splints from the constant pounding on the cinders.

Emboldened by victory after victory, as the season wore on, our resolve was to stay undefeated and we almost did. Our only setback was the fourth place finish at the State Meet, a meet always dominated by the New York City and Long Island schools, where a 10.0 flat 100 was commonplace.

One night during the summer of 2002, over dinner, I was reliving my past glory and showed the old track photographs to my friend Jim Hughes, a photographer. I mentioned that all the guys still lived in Auburn. One thing led to another, and Jim and I decided it would be a great idea to get the crew together for a repeat photograph - while we still could!

"Let's set the guys up in the same place and in the same order as in the 1957 photo," Jim suggested. The next morning I got on the phone and started making arrangements.

Everyone was agreeable and Butch typically said, "That's cool."

So on a warm September morning in 2002, there we were again at Holland Stadium. After some back pats, old stories, and many laughs, we got down to business with Jim. We did the photo shoot, trying to recreate that moment in 1957. Someone suggested that we really run the relay one more time for old times' sake. Butch, never hesitating to meet a challenge, said, "Let's get it on." Obviously, he hadn't changed much.

It took Tom, the intellectual of the group, to remind the rest of the old-timers that discretion is the better part of valor. Just as well. It was too nice a day to hobble home with a "charley horse" and, besides, we weren't ready to meet our Maker, just yet.

Instead of actually running, we enjoyed some more good-humored banter and good-natured ribbing, relived the unbridled joy we felt after setting the Section III record and satisfied ourselves with the posed pictures.

It was great seeing my teammates together again as a unit, but it seemed a little strange standing next to these three other old fellows and imagining the youngsters we once were.

As Chuckles got into his car, he yelled over his shoulder, "Won't it be fun to do this again in twenty years?"

"Right!" we replied in unison.

Note: Included are four photographs, two from 1957 and two more from September, 2002, reposing the old black & whites.

1957 Team

Left To Right—Butch, Chuckles,

Mercury, Bo.

95

"Same Pose—2002"

Handoff from me to Chuckles. After a successful handoff (barely), I did a nosedive into the track, sliding on the cinders. The Hydrogen Peroxide used to clean my wounds stung like a swarm of bees.

"Same Pose—2002"

15

TALL TALES

As a high school student back in the fifties, I played football on Auburn's varsity team. We were a good team and I got my fifteen minutes of fame while playing against one of our toughest rivals, Elmira Free Academy, on our home field.

Elmira had a great running back named Ernie Davis. Ernie stood about 6'2" and was an imposing figure at 210 pounds. He was known as the "Elmira Express" because he literally ran over any obstacle in his way. Davis went on to become an All-American at Syracuse University and to win the Heisman Trophy (1961).

I stood 5'8" and weighed 155 pounds. From my position at right defensive end, I saw my worst nightmare each time I looked at Ernie.

On one play, I shed his lead blocker, as Ernie headed off left tackle. Fate had put me in the right place at the right time to be an obstacle in Ernie's path. Due to fear or panic, I hit him low, around the ankles, so as not to get in the way of those muscular thighs. After Ernie got up, he limped off the field. Davis had been badly shaken by my tackle, and the half time score seemed to show it.

I was exhilarated in the locker room when coach Dean said, "The way to tackle a back of Ernie's size and ability is to hit him like Bob did. Hit him low."

Although we were on the short side of a 7-6 score, we no longer felt intimidated by Davis...until shortly after the second half began.

Apparently we didn't hit the elusive halfback at all during our second half calamity, because the final score was 33-12, indicating a thorough thumping.

I never told Coach that I was just trying to avoid getting killed in my encounter with Davis. I have told that story several times to anyone who would listen, but I change it a little each time. The last time I simply said, "I hit him low and he limped off the field."

Sometimes the less said the better.

I had one other opportunity for glory, this time on offense.

We were playing Ithaca High School on their home field. I was playing right end when my number was called for a square-in pass from the Ithaca ten-yard line. Our quarterback had confidence in me because I had had a fantastic week of practice—I caught everything thrown my way. His pass was perfect, hitting me right in the hands, but before I could safely tuck the ball away, I collided with "Turtle," our left end who had run the wrong pattern, I think. I fell helplessly to the turf as the ball bounced away.

The last time I told the story I said, "If it wasn't for Turtle slamming into me, I would have caught the winning touchdown pass."

On October 16, 2003 I was in a restaurant and I heard a man tell his daughter something that sums up pretty much the way things are with former athletes. He said, "The older I get, the better I was."

"I Hope I Don't Get Killed."

16

DEBATE

After the Elmira Free Academy game, our stellar running back, my friend Tony, collared me in the locker room and complained that I had ruined his touchdown run in the second half because I had clipped an Elmira player. Tony's touchdown was called back, and we were given a fifteen yard penalty from which we never recovered.

In my defense, I told Tony that he scored only because I had clipped the defensive player in the first place. He asked, "What do you mean?" I just walked away. Can you believe that he still complains about the clip, some forty years later?

Athletes, football players in particular, are always arguing about whether you win games with offense or with defense. I tried to use logic while explaining to Tony why games are won with defense. As former tailbacks usually do, he took the opposite view.

I said, "Tony, I can prove that you win with defense."

"Yeah," he said, "I'm listening."

"If your team scores a touchdown, can you still lose the game?" I asked.

"Yeah," he said, and continued with, "but that's no proof."

"Right," I said, "but if you are never scored upon, can you ever lose the game?"

"I guess not," he said.

"See," I said, "you win with defense."

Tony pondered that for a moment and then said, "You know Bob, you have the uncanny ability to state the obvious in clandestine terms."

"What?" I said.

He just walked away.

I went to my room, got my dictionary and looked up "clandestine." This former athlete was now becoming an intellectual.

Tony and I frequently engage in playful banter. We recently played a round of golf in which he shot his usual low 70s score and I shot my usual high number. In a moment of inspiration he said, "Bob, what happened to you?"

"What do you mean, Tony?"

"You used to be a good athlete," he said.

"Life got in the way," I explained. "I'm not like you; your most complicated thought is how high to tee-up the golf ball."

Ignoring my insult, "Let's have a brew," he said. "You're buying."

17

FUHGEDDABOUDIT

In addition to Tony we had some other characters on that team. They would try anything to get the edge on an opponent.

Two of those characters were brothers, Gino and Bruno. They played right next to me, at right guard and right tackle. We were getting ready to play perennial power Rome Free Academy at Holland Stadium. The brothers devised a scheme by which they would give their blocking assignments in Italian. They put their ingenious plan to work play after play. But to no avail. Nothing worked.

Rome trounced us, and the right side of our offensive line was totally ineffective. After the game Gino and Bruno, being good-natured fellas, met with the defensive guard and defensive tackle from Rome to congratulate them on the great game they played.

Gino said, "Hi, I'm Gino."

Bruno said, "Hi, I'm Bruno."

The two boys from Rome first smirked, and then smiled as they said, "Hi, I'm Vito," and "Hi, I'm Guido." As they walked away, they turned and said, *"Hey paisans, fuhgeddaboudit. Quando Ritornarete a Roma il prossimo anno, we will kick your ass again."*

Our boys took a ribbing for weeks afterward.

One wise guy gave each of them an Italian dictionary.

BOOK IV

TEACHING

18

MIXED COMMUNICATION

Teachers are often asked to perform some task, only to be ordered to do just the opposite the next day.

One day a new guidance counselor sent me a note explaining that a student, Eddie Gobel, should be added to my study hall list.

Being the conscientious employee that I was, I patiently checked each day for Eddie's arrival. Several days passed and Eddie had still not shown up, although other teachers had spotted him in school, so I sought out the counselor, and the following dialogue occurred:

Counselor: "How can I help you?"

Me: "Eddie Gobel…"

Counselor: "Hi, Eddie! Nice to meet you."

Me: "I'm not Eddie! I'm Bob Calimeri. You sent me an add slip for Eddie Gobel, but he has never appeared in class."

Counselor: "Gee, that's too bad. Why don't you find out where he is and get back to me on that."

116

Me: "Get back to you? Why do you think I came down here in the first place?"

And so it goes some days in public education, where accountability can be suspect and responsibilities are easily confused.

As I had done so many other times in my tenure, I chalked it up to experience and moved on.

19

A GREAT MAN OF SHORT STATURE

I had a wonderful time teaching biology, especially genetics and reproduction. My classes were lively and I was full of energy. The kids were respectful and even called me mister, as in Mr. C, or Mr. Calimeri. Over the years those references have evolved into some really imaginative epithets, many unprintable. It's really amazing how creative young minds can be. That's societal evolution for you.

Prior to 1970, there were three high schools in Auburn, East, West and Central. In 1970 these schools were combined into one big, brand new school, Auburn High School. That fusion, plus the fact that the parochial high school, Mount Carmel, finally closed its doors after twelve years, swelled the AHS population to 2700 students.

At the time, educational philosophy had evolved into the "bigger is better" thing. Integrating the three schools into one huge building was a double-edged sword. On the one hand the science labs were amazing and we had a great

118

football team (I used to kid Coach Adams that he never had to give a motivational speech at half time because he was usually ahead by 30 or more points).

On the other hand, kids lost the personal touch that only a small school can provide. To the old cliché regarding the only two certainties in life, death and taxes, I would add a third item, the universal quest by teen-agers to be noticed. "You can be nice to me, you can be mean to me, but please *notice* me," are implicit phrases in most adolescent thought.

I recently read that the current thinking is "smaller is better." We do that a lot in education, travel in circles. But, no one will dispute the fact that it is easier to make friends and be noticed in a small school rather than in a large school.

The enormous size of Auburn High School provided me the opportunity to strut my stuff. In addition to several coaching awards presented to me over the years, the two awards that I treasure most are not associated with athletics.

In 1974 I happened to be in the right place at the right time. There was a near-riot at the school, involving non-lethal weapons like fists and chains, and I was instrumental in isolating the leader from his posse, thus possibly preventing a violent outcome. For that I was awarded an "Outstanding Secondary Educators of America" award, an award originating out of Washington, D.C. I'm looking at the handsome paperweight right now.

WSTM-TV, Channel 3 presented "Educator of the Week," the second award, to me in June of 2002. Two students from Tyburn Academy, that small school where I teach part-time and where the students often genuflect when they see me, nominated me for that award. I'm looking at the handsome plaque right now.

So it appears that within a span of 28 years, I haven't lost my touch after all. Maybe teaching part-time has been good for me.

Getting back to the early years at AHS, I continued to teach biology until 1975, when an opening occurred in the math department. I think I was getting stale, because I found myself teaching without really engaging my brain. That can happen, you know, talking by rote. One time a student who had to repeat biology said, "Hey 'Teach,' you said exactly the same thing last year."

"Yes, I was hoping that this year you might listen even better," I said.

But he may have had a point, so I jumped at the chance to transfer to math.

Subsequent to my transfer from the science department to the math department, my closest friends in the science department, Mike and Rocco, spread the word that the IQ of both departments had gone up. I still don't get it, but I did hear that the math people were furious for some reason. When I asked them what was wrong, they just gave me dirty looks. Poor sports, I guess.

No one better personifies the greatness of the everyday teacher than my good friend Rocco, a veteran of 34 years in public schools, and still going strong. Always quick with a quip, he loves the kids and the kids love him. Although he is a little short for his height, he knows all the ins and outs of the game and has a story to illustrate any educational principle.

A few years after the ultimate Cinderella story "Rocky" was released as a motion picture, Rocco informed me that henceforth he wanted to be called Rocky, as in Rocky Balboa, the mythical boxer who attained the pinnacle of pugilism when he became heavyweight champion of the world.

When I asked him why he wanted the name change, he enthusiastically said, "Rocky was the underdog and a nobody who through hard work and dedication reached the ultimate in his profession. Bo, I too feel as though I have scaled many mountains and overcome many obstacles to get where I am today."

"Rock," I said, "you've only been teaching a few years; how can you have reached the summit already?"

"I'm precocious. You've always said so yourself."

"That may be true, little buddy, but you'll always be Rocco to me. I love you just the way you are."

He was angry for a while, but he got over it as he always does.

Rocco eschews educational gobbledygook and cuts to heart of the matter on any issue. Ask him a question and you will likely get a lively monologue punctuated with names, dates, and places. He forgets not a detail. Rocco has seen it all, done it all, and has it all catalogued in his encyclopedic memory.

There are things I have done to Rocco over the years that I regret, like the time I walked into his room while he was lecturing and asked: "Hey, Rock, are you standing up?" His students burst out laughing and he threw me a look full of daggers. That was really not a nice thing to do to someone who is vertically challenged. When Rocco's wife, Jan, heard about my mischief, she sent me a nasty e-mail, which I immediately deleted before some of my Christian friends saw it.

Sometimes the temptation was so great, that I couldn't resist zinging him. It's an aspect of my adolescent days, which I hope to outgrow some day. Rocco says that I am suffering from "arrested-development syndrome."

Rocco is really lucky, I mean horseshoe lucky. One time many, many years ago I was working as a playground director at West High School playground, and Rocco was one of my charges. Even though only a few years separated our ages, we enjoyed playing horseshoes together. On one occasion, I had just released the horseshoe when his mom yelled "Rocco" from the front porch of their nearby home. He was distracted just enough to lose sight of the flight of the incoming horseshoe. It was just a glancing blow to his skull, but to this day, he maintains that I was a ventriloquist.

Before he received the horseshoe headache, Rocco had some peculiar tendencies. After his recovery he was the most normal kid you would ever want to meet. It was as though he had been transformed by a successful brain operation.

Another game Rocco and I enjoy playing was chess. My victories were few, buy after his transformation at the age of twelve, I never won another game, and he never let me forget about it.

He asked me one day: "Bobby, where does our next thought come from?" He had me there. I couldn't think of a thing to say. He was really precocious like that.

The other day my wife and I were having dinner with Rocco and Jan. We were reminiscing about our playground days and I recounted the story of his "precocious" comment. Once again, he transformed himself into "genius" mode and uttered this mind-game query: "If we really knew where our next thought came from, would life be over in an instant?" Rocco hasn't changed much over the years, and apparently neither have I.

As the saying goes, "Great minds often come in small packages." Rocco, is living proof of that, as were Toulouse-Lautrec, Napoleon, and Tom Thumb.

On another occasion, during those playground days, I tried to get even with Rocco for some prank he had played on me. I told him to play second base during one of our inter-playground baseball games. When he took his position, he yelled back to me, "Hey coach, where's the base?"

"You're it," I said.

That was the perfect squelch, because for once he had no retort. Instead, he tried to resort to violence, but because he was a bit roly-poly, he never laid a glove on me as he chased me all around the field.

His brothers, Vinny and Ant'ny used to "scorch" him on a daily basis. He would chase them all over the playground as well, but he never caught them either, even though they were running backwards.

One ritual that Rocco and I used to perform years ago on the playground was pitching and catching. Since he was a "lefty," he thought he had a natural curve ball, which was, and still is, the hope of every adolescent who ever played the game of baseball. Rocco would pitch the ball and yell, "Did it curve, Bob?"

And I would always respond with the same refrain, "Yeah, it curved, Rock," and then I would add under my breath, "straight as an arrow."

Recently our two families got together to enjoy Rocco's delicious homemade pizza, and he was bragging about his curve ball. I just let it ride because I didn't want to burst the bubble in front of his boys.

Rocco and I have some good golfing buddies. One time Rocco, Rick, Vinnie-Three-Times (we called him that because he always wanted two Mulligans on the first tee), and I were enjoying a sunny day on the links. Just as I was beginning my down swing, Rocco dropped his pants. Out of the corner of my eye I saw his pants on their way south. My game fell apart as my ball took a perfect 90-degree turn and landed far into the woods. Rick got spastic and Vinnie's game fell apart. Also, our designated caddie, Louie, fell out of the golf cart in a fit of uncontrollable laughter. All Rocco could say was, "Now we're even." I still don't get it. Even for what?

We were always doing stuff like that, becoming more like our students every day. Evidently we've learned as much from them as they have learned from us.

I've cherished all the moments I have had with my good buddy, even though he recently hurt my feelings.

On two occasions over the past four years I developed a serious case of Bells Palsy. On the first occasion, my right eye became fixed and the right side of my face fell and was paralyzed for several months. On the second occasion, the paralysis struck the left side. My friends, led by Rocco, referred to me as Quasi (as in Quasimoto), Igor, and Popeye. Unbeknownst to me, to add insult to injury, Rocco had ten place mats made with an image of my distorted face on them, and at the opportune moment at Michael's restaurant, my favorite watering hole, all ten of my so-called friends raised the mats high and sang "Happy Birthday." Everybody in the restaurant clapped. I was totally embarrassed. To this day, Rocco has shown no remorse for his hurtful misdeed.

Although we have been friends for 45 years, he pushed his luck a bit with the restaurant stunt. But I got over it. I responded the same way I did in order to survive three decades in the classroom—I pouted and overate for a week.

"Sorry Rocco!"

"I Can, I Can, I Know I Can!"

"Fore!"

20

RELEVANCY

The concept of relevancy is frequently foremost in the minds of students. There is no good answer to the query, "Why do I need to know this or that?"

I knew this question would come up because I had been warned by experts that "students will unintentionally suck out all your marrow and leave your bones hollow and brittle if you let them" (sometimes it is intentional). So, after many years of responding to this question with clever things like "because I said so," I finally decided to say, "I'm putting tools into your toolbox."

One day the perfect opportunity to employ the "toolbox" scenario arose. When I asked the kid with a safety pin through his eyebrow if he was concerned about infection, he said, "My philosophy is 'no fear,' and that's why I'm going to be a cop, dude."

I couldn't argue with that, but then he asked, "Why are you teaching me this math-stuff which I ain't ever gonna use?"

"Algebra will help in the development of your reasoning skills," I said, and followed with my brilliant statement, "I'm just putting tools into your toolbox. Some of these tools will never be used, but isn't it better to be prepared in case you need one?"

I was on a roll now, so I said, "Look, suppose you go for a walk on a cloudy day and you take your umbrella with you as a precaution. If it doesn't rain, you have lost nothing, and you may have even strengthened your arm. If it rains, you won't get wet."

I did it; I was so proud that I had finally transferred a concept I had learned in a workshop to the classroom.

The boy looked at me and said, "I don't go for no walks." I decided not to reveal the rest of my words of wisdom because I knew it would be useless and boring to him. I had been prepared to say:

> If we had a crystal ball to see the future, we probably wouldn't need all the tools in the toolbox; we could simply pick and choose. Unfortunately, that is not the case.

Anyway, a crystal ball precludes surprises and spontaneity, usually one of life's fun things. My theory is really very simple. It's nice to know something so that when you're out on a date eating pizza and drinking soda, you can say more than, 'Hey, man, what's happ'nin'?'

Do you remember the song that had a line that went 'With all the crap I learned in high school it's a wonder I can think at all?' Since you can't think in a vacuum, you should feel fortunate that someone tried to fill your toolbox.

Near the end of my teaching career, when I was obviously tired and worn out, I could always count on at least one student each day to be obnoxious, like the time I sent a student into the hall because he was being very disruptive. I allowed him to return a few minutes before the end of class to get his homework assignment. He said, "You know where this shoe is going?" as he pointed to his foot.

Expecting the obvious, I said, "No, tell me."

"On this chair," he responded.

When I told this comedian, on another occasion, that he was digging himself a deep hole, he said, "That can't be, because I don't have a shovel." I couldn't argue with that. Not only did he have no shovel; the poor kid had almost no tools at all.

There were two incidents that put the final nails in my teaching coffin.

The first incident happened while I was teaching a sixth-grade class during the summer of 1996. On the last day of class, as I approached a misbehaving student, he said, "Don't touch me fat ass or I'll punch your lights out!" I was really bothered by the "fat" part, because I had been on a diet that apparently wasn't working.

I had officially retired in June, and I was still being abused in August.

The second incident allowed me to use my best Robert DeNiro impression. Two students were standing toe-to-toe in the hallway. I approached them and said, "Looks like a confrontation going on here—be on your way."

"There ain't no confrontation going one here; but if it becomes one, I'll call you," said the taller of the two.

Then that famous line from "Taxi Driver" popped into my head, so I said, "You talkin' to me?" as I gestured with my hands.

"Yeah, I'm talkin' to you," he retorted.

I wrote the kid up, but as usual nothing much happened to him outside of a little psychological counseling.

Hopefully, as teen-agers mature they will go on to lead productive lives. A former high school teacher, now a TV personality, recently said, "I was a cut-up in school—a real wise-guy, and I sat in the row for dummies. And I turned out O.K."

It's amazing how new-found maturity and the school of hard-knocks can turn one's life around.

When I think about the rudeness I endured during the waning years of my tenure, I reflected on a lecture by Pulitzer Prize-winner Frank McCourt, author of <u>Angela's Ashes</u>. McCourt spent 30 years in the trenches of New York City schools. Bless the teachers who work in inner-city schools like those in New York, Philadelphia and Chicago.

Insolence, boredom, whining and *grumbling* were adjectives McCourt used when describing his students. They had an infinite number of strategies to drive a weak teacher from the planet…and some strong teachers, too. A timid teacher had no chance of success. Educators who work in these environments age more quickly than teachers who work in small-city districts or rural communities.

This situation reminds me of the growth of plants. The old leaves at the bottom of the plant wither and die first so that the newly emerging leaves at the top can gain sustenance and grow. This is nature's way.

There are two sides to the teaching coin. In describing his experience McCourt said that on good days he was anxious to get started, but on bad days "I wanted to put a pin through my brain."

Some mornings his students appeared to be sleepwalking, while after lunch they enjoyed self-imposed siesta time.

He had to wear many hats—"those of scholar, counselor, pediatrician, drill sergeant, and song-and-dance man."

McCourt concluded by saying that through all of the tumult, "When you make a breakthrough, there is something that happens that is absolutely mystical."

That helps to sustain you, but ultimately you are on a one-way trip, like the old leaves at the bottom of the plant.

"I Fear Nothing!"

21

INNOVATION

A few years before I retired I attended a workshop in which we were told to make the classroom resemble the home, within reason—nice and comfortable. We were told to bring in rugs and furniture. I always tried to stay abreast of new innovations in education, so I brought in a plaid chair, mostly orange, that was in good shape. The student who got the highest grade on my weekly test was allowed to sit in the chair for a week. The kids really liked this idea. When I was observed for evaluation purposes, I made sure to point out the chair to the administrator. One time after a really hard class, I decided to sit for a few minutes in that comfortable, orange chair before my next class, which was located in another room. Fifteen minutes later, a colleague, another math teacher, awakened me. Marge said, "Bob, don't you have a class now?"

"Yes," I said, "but the bell hasn't rung yet, has it?"

"It rang about ten minutes ago," she replied.

For about a week afterwards, my colleagues would ask, "Hey Bob, how's the chair?" Sometimes, there were administrators present when they asked that question.

On August 9, 2002, ten years after the chair incident, I ran into a former student. We exchanged some good-natured banter about this and that. As she was leaving, she looked over her shoulder and said, "Hey, Mr. Cal, how's the chair?" We both laughed.

The next stop for that orange chair was an apartment at the other end of the state, where my son lived when he was a college student.

That was ten years ago. From there, I know not where it went.

"Oh, Bob!"

22

ON THE INSIDE

Occasionally an opportunity arises that is referred to in educational circles as a "teaching moment." Since it is fleeting and ephemeral, it is absolutely essential that the teacher recognizes it, seizes it, and gets the most out of it.

One such moment occurred when I was teaching mathematics at Auburn Correctional Facility (they don't call it a prison anymore). As I went through those metal doors for the first time and heard them clang shut behind me, I was scared, really scared. My foreboding was caused by every prison movie I had ever seen, especially the ones starring James Cagney.

During break-time on the first night of class, I got into what I thought was a good-natured discussion on why it is important to study math. I decided not to use my "toolbox" analogy because I knew these folks wouldn't be out walking in the rain any time soon.

I concluded the discussion with, "By studying math you will be able to determine the number of years you have left on your sentence."

In retrospect, I don't think I would say that again, but fortunately no one seemed to take offense, and one of the inmates said, "Hey Teach, tell us a story."

So I did. I regaled them with a story about my physical education teacher, Ed, and how he punished me. I told them how he gave me a stinging whack on my ass with his heavy oak paddle for breaking one of his rules—don't talk in the hall on the way outdoors for gym class. I told them how I remember silently saying to myself, "Thank you sir; may I please have another." His rule was designed so that we wouldn't disturb classes that were in session. The thing is, the students respected Ed, even though he was tough on us, because we knew he cared about our well-being as well as the well-being of everyone else in the school. Funny thing, I never talked in the hall again on my way outdoors for gym class. He had made a lasting impression on my psyche as well as on my butt.

Ed was never sued, and I never told my parents, for obvious reasons.

"I wonder what would happen to him if the incident occurred today?" I inquired of my attentive audience.

The only response I got was silence and blank stares. I assumed they weren't impressed, so I resumed teaching the math lesson.

It was a long time before I attempted to take advantage of a "teaching moment" again. I just didn't feel confident.

Actually, my career at the correctional facility almost ended before it began. On that first day I wore lightweight yellow pants, because nobody told me not to. It had been a very warm evening.

As the group of teachers and our supervisor crossed the main yard, a storm of jeers, wolf whistles and catcalls were directed toward me. I really didn't know what was happening until the supervisor informed me that yellow was the color of the raincoats worn by the extraction team. The inmates referred to that team as the "goon" squad. I had naively thought that the inmates liked my tight yellow pants for other reasons. By then, the damage had been done.

My tenure at the facility came to an abrupt end after three years. One evening, because of trouble in the main yard, the teachers were asked to evacuate the school. We were temporarily herded into a small room with a glass front. As the inmates were exiting the building, one of them looked directly at me and I saw him mouth the words, "I'm going to take you hostage," and then he laughed.

I decided not to push my luck, so I quit at the end of the year.

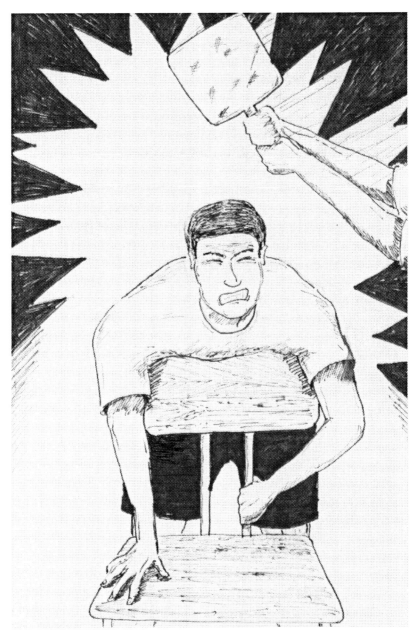

"Thank You Sir; May I Please Have Another?"

23

DUKE AND ME

Although I wasn't a very imposing and intimidating physical specimen, I could usually outwit my students.

I had been teaching biology at the time of the incident. Several students, including Duke, the toughest kid in the class, were talking loudly and creating a distraction. I wanted to convey to all of my students that I was completely in charge. I selected Duke to serve as an object lesson for the class. Duke was an intimidating figure. With huge shoulders attached to tree-trunk-like arms, and a tiny waist, he resembled the popular image of Paul Bunyan. Also, since Duke had been giving me a lot of grief for many days, he was the appropriate tool for this lesson.

"Duke," I said, "get your butt into the prep-room." The prep-room was located through a door at the front of my classroom. As Duke swaggered up the aisle and through the door, I swaggered right behind him. There was absolute silence as we walked, the students sensing the danger. Once in the prep-room, I instructed Duke to exit into the hallway through another door and go to the principal's office.

Then, I simulated all hell breaking loose in the prep-room. I kicked over boxes of books, broke a beaker, and did other things to indicate that Duke and I were having a showdown. After the mayhem had subsided, the ominous silence in the prep-room seemed to suggest a fatal outcome.

My students, who were expecting the victorious Duke to come through the door to inform them of my death, were absolutely flabbergasted when I entered the room with a wide grin on my face while rubbing my hands together, indicating a job well-done. They were then certain that the big guy was dead, and they wondered who would be next.

When Duke, who had been sent home by the principal, showed up for school the next day, the students knew that they had been had. The lesson was, "Don't trifle with Mr. C."

However, they did get even. The case of the missing grasshopper was evidence that those biology students held a grudge. Although I was pretty alert during biology lab, one day I must have dropped my guard. A grasshopper was stolen from my lab and showed up as an ingredient in the school principal's spinach soup at lunch that day. She evidently failed to see the humor in the event, because when her subsequent investigation led to miscreants under my charge in my biology lab, I was required to attend a workshop on laboratory supervision. My friends in the department said that both the crime and the punishment made their day.

The following day, when the laughter had subsided, the students and I called it a draw, made a truce, and lived in peace for the rest of the year.

"Move It Big Boy!"

24

GO TO SCHOOL

The other day a young student of mine at Tyburn Academy showed me a picture of his car. I said that it was really nice looking and continued with, "Since you have such a great set of wheels, why are you late for school almost every day?" He had no reasonable answer. I then proceeded to tell him a story.

When I was in the tenth grade, I made it a point to always be on time for school, I told him. However, one day I was unavoidably late. As I entered the building, the only sound I heard was the rapid beating of my heart, because I knew that I would be coming face-to-face with Mr. Kelly (we called him "Bo," but not to his face, of course). Bo was the highly respected principal of the school at the time. He was a model leader, a strict disciplinarian, who conveyed his message by simply looking at you. As I entered the main office, the sight of him caused my heart rate to accelerate even more. He looked me straight in the eye, never said a word, and gave me a tardy pass. I was never late again.

161

The boy I had been trying to impress with the story looked at me kind of funny, as though something wasn't right with me. "What's your point?" he said.

Seeing that he wasn't impressed with that story, I tried another one to get him to understand that students should go to school all the time, unless they are sick. I recalled, with some humor, a particular day in my young life when I didn't want to go to school. I was in the eighth grade and I had worked until midnight as a "pin boy" at the old Roman Bowling Lanes on Clark Street, and I was understandably tired. My older and wiser brother, Jerry, said, "You're going to school!" He proceeded to rip the covers off of me, grab me by the ankles, and pull me off the bed. I banged my head on the floor and was a hurting puppy during my one-mile walk to school. After hearing this story, all the boy wanted to know was if I went to the nurse's office when I got to school. Sometimes, I do have trouble getting my point across.

"Nice Wheels, Man."

25

SCARY MOMENTS

As a new teacher I was pretty unsure of myself. A former teacher had told me that it would probably take me five years to become really comfortable with what I was doing. I had no problem with the subject matter in biology, but on the few occasions when I did, I told the students to look up the material because "research is good for you." The other trick I employed was to ask the smartest kid in the class to give an explanation.

Although those were merely anxious moments, occasionally really scary moments occurred. The scariest teaching moment for me occurred during my rookie year. During biology lab the students were doing a blood-typing exercise and I was sitting at my desk observing. The students were working in pairs, pricking each other's finger with a lancet to get a few drops of blood. Suddenly, one of the macho boys in the corner of the room disappeared behind a lab table. I won't be fooled by this little charade, I thought, because I had read in Education 101 about the stunts kids will pull on new teachers. Although the students acted really concerned, some even screaming, I didn't pay them any mind because I knew they were all in cahoots.

After three or four minutes he still hadn't popped up. I began to question my analysis of the situation, so with my heart racing I went to his lab table. Sure enough, he was out cold. After sending for the nurse, I put cold compresses on his neck and forehead. Although he had apparently fainted, the nurse quickly revived him. He was more embarrassed than hurt. Boy, was I glad to see him return to the land of the living, but for a moment I thought that I had witnessed my first fatality. Those labs are not generally done anymore because of the danger of hepatitis and other uncomfortable things.

Another scary moment occurred when I was walking down the hall of my alma mater, where I was then teaching. Suddenly, I heard someone cry out in a tiny voice, "Help me! Help me!" like the human/fly hybrid I had seen in a movie on television. I followed the direction of the plea and eventually stood opposite a student locker. Self-consciously, I spoke to the locker. I asked, "Are you in there?"

I was startled when the locker answered me. "Yes," it said. "Please get me out of here."

I found out later that some boys had stuffed little Joanne into her own locker.

Joanne was the smallest girl in her class and a timid little mouse. This was not the first time she had been picked on. Although she was terrified, she refused to identify the boys who had done it. What's interesting is that soon after that incident, a small group of boys became Joanne's protectors for the rest of the year. I firmly believe that they were actually the perpetrators, and because she had not "ratted" on them, she became part of their group.

26

MRS. DIDDLE

Mrs. Diddle, my former colleague, was no schoolmarm from the old school. She always tried to stay current in her thinking and creative in her health classes, sometimes too creative.

Veteran teachers generally lived by the credo: "Don't smile until Christmas...otherwise, they will eat you up." Personally, if I was sure that I had complete control, I usually cracked a smile by November 1.

I never did figure out when Mrs. Diddle celebrated Christmas.

Although she was stern in appearance and had a reputation of being a "task-master," in reality she was a very caring person. However, the caring part of her personality was seldom appreciated until years later. I have run into many of her former students over the years and they all say basically the same thing: "You know Mr. C, I always suffered from mild anxiety in Mrs. D's class and I didn't care for her teaching style. But from my current vantage point as an adult, I realize how effective she was."

I would always respond with, "My, you have become wise over the years."

While she often used charts, models and other typical props in her classes, Mrs. Diddle insisted that each of her students bring in a banana for "Banana Day," a day when she appeared uncharacteristically nervous.

One day I heard a student utter, "Hey, Claude, are you going to Diddle's class today?"

"Are you kidding me or what?" said Claude. "Did you forget that today is Banana Day? I wouldn't miss it for the world."

"Okay boys and girls," said Mrs. Diddle, "those of you who are right-handed, hold the banana in your left hand and vice versa. Now carefully put it over the top of the banana and gently unroll it all the way to the bottom."

"Hey, does anyone want to trade my red one for a blue one?" said one of the outgoing girls who seemed to enjoy her brief excursion into naughtiness. With that the class cracked up and all was lost. Although every year someone interjected a comment that would crack the class up, Mrs.

Diddle forged ahead, doing her part for posterity. She told me that Banana Day was the only day of the year in which she had perfect attendance in all of her classes.

Although today's educators are expected to be all things to all students, from psychiatrists to mechanics, there is a great deal of humor to sustain them. Mrs. Diddle provided, although unintentionally, some of that humor.

"I Must Keep A Straight Face."

27

DON'T BLINK

The school hallway was sometimes the worst place for anyone who valued his life. I remember one incident that happened when I was supervising the corridor outside my room between classes. I was located at the intersection of two corridors and it was about twenty seconds before the tardy bell. Suddenly, a large, burly football player came flying down one of the halls as though he were in the last few yards of a touchdown run, and he was about to make a right-hand turn around the corner. Coming down the other hall, and just about to turn the corner was a petite freshman girl clutching a load of books to her breast. I knew that the inevitable was about to happen, and that I was helpless to prevent it. Just as I began to yell a warning, the two students turned the corner simultaneously.

The collision was horrific. Books and papers exploded in all directions. She ended up flying several yards backward before landing on her rear end. Fortunately, she was not injured, probably because she was walking relaxed and shielded by her load of books. I think she was more embarrassed than anything else. The boy stopped momentarily to say he was sorry and then continued running to class. He left her sitting there, dazed, with books lying all around her. I surmised that only one thing could turn a decent human being into such a thoughtless lout—he didn't want to be late for Mrs. Diddle's class, since it was Banana Day.

Later, as I thought about it, I figured that if I had blinked, I would have missed the whole thing.

"I Can Make It!"

28

FUN ACTIVITY

At the start of a new school year, I always try to get to know my students very quickly. One time I tried to establish rapport by coaching a small group in the intricacies of juggling. One of my prize students was Ali. She was introverted and I wanted her to come out of her shell. I recalled that my former track star, Kathy, had reminded me that repetition was important, if you wanted to get good at something. So, Ali and I worked very hard, every day for one month, on juggling exercises.

One afternoon, as Ali was leaving school, I casually and jokingly told her that she was accomplished enough at juggling to go home and juggle her mother's cups.

The next day I got a phone call from Ali's mother. Instead of thanking me for taking the time to help her daughter with a fun activity, all she wanted to know was how she was going to replace the two new china cups that Ali dropped while following my suggestion.

"At least she caught one of them," I said glibly.

To say she was angry would be to put it mildly. Instead of appreciating my humor, she slammed the phone in my ear.

Some people have no sense of humor.

From that day forward, I was very cautious when working with teen-agers. I no longer wanted to say or do anything that would come back to haunt me.

"I'm Dead Meat Now!"

29

HEART ATTACK

The unpredictability of teen-agers never ceased to amaze me. Shortly after I retired, I was temporarily employed as a long-term substitute at West Genesee High School in Syracuse. As expected, the assignment was not easy. I had many behavior problems, compounded by the fact that I was a substitute. To many students, "substitute" is synonymous with "a person to be tested."

Even my study hall gave me trouble, except for the set of twins, Patsy and Catherine. They were courteous and kind and had a great sense of humor. Among the boys, Chris was the most obnoxious, needing the last word under all circumstances. He would often mock me. I hesitated to send him to the office, because I didn't want to be known as the retired teacher who couldn't handle a class, but Chris was becoming a real problem in my life.

One evening I wasn't feeling well, but I decided to wait until morning before determining whether or not to go to work. Since I felt better in the morning, I went in. My first two classes went okay, but during my third period study hall I began to sweat and I was having trouble with my speech. In a fog, I got up and started for the door. I remember beginning to fall, and the next thing I knew I was lying on the floor. Surrounding me were three wonderful women, one of whom was the school nurse. "To what do I owe this pleasant surprise?" I asked. The nurse informed me that someone from my class had called the nurse's office to report that I had had a heart attack. She then smiled and said that the medics were on the way.

At the hospital, I experienced a battery of tests with no definite diagnosis. The ER doctor surmised that I was developing the flu and had become dehydrated. I took the next day off from work and then got right back into it. During third period I approached the twins to thank them for saving my life. "Mr. Cal, it wasn't us. It was him," they said, as they pointed to Chris.

Knowing in my heart that my secret wish for Chris to be transformed into a human being after all had come true, I approached him with a broad smile on my face, held out my hand, and thanked him profusely. He glanced at me with a puzzled look on his face.

"Whatever," he said, ignoring my outstretched hand. The next day in class he was his old self. So was I.

For weeks afterward, as I walked down the hall, I would hear the kids say, "Hey, there's the teacher who had the heart attack." Although that certainly wasn't true, I will concede that I did have a mild "attack of the heart" for one day.

"He's Not Dead Yet."

30

SELF-ESTEEM

After school one day, I joined up with Mike, David and Rocco for a round of golf. After a hard day in the classroom, we found that playing golf helped us to release stress.

Following a series of slices, hooks, dubs, and whiffs, we started to talk shop. The conversation soon came around to the concept of *self-esteem*, a very popular topic among educators over the last decade or so. It seems many people believe a student will learn more efficiently if *we* can just somehow inflate his or her self-image. A National Education Association resolution urges that curricula be designed to "foster positive self-esteem." Some schools have even designated a "Self-Esteem Day," assuming that one day's activities can somehow elevate a student's self-image simply by talking about it.

Rocco, gazing through the spectacles of experience, thinks this "feel-good" mentality, praising without real cause to do so, is not the answer. According to him, genuine positive feelings can be attained only through effective analytical thinking and the constructive efforts a student is willing to make toward some positive goal. In short, no one can give you self-esteem; it must be earned.

"Besides," said Rocco, "why does everyone worry endlessly about the self-esteem of the students and never that of the teachers? Their self-images take a daily pounding, but there is a solution. One must be able to handle a negative situation and turn it into a positive."

Rocco was just warming up.

He then launched into his monologue. "Last week one of the boys in my class, who was doing poorly, said, 'Mr. L., I don't understand you one-hundred percent of the time, but last year I didn't understand Mr. P. two-hundred percent of the time.'" The kid then snickered, "Your subject is irrelevant anyway." Rocco pondered this. The only thing he could come up with was that he was twice as good as Mr. P. on the delivery of irrelevant material. But that made him feel pretty good.

He then related another recent incident. At the end of one semester, Rocco gave a student an "incomplete" because he had missed a test.

The student, hopping mad, repeated over and over again, "I don't want no incomplete. Don't give me no incomplete."

So Rocco calculated the boy's grade with the 0 figured in and gave him a final grade of 55%.

Still not satisfied, the student continued shouting at Rocco, "You suck as a teacher; you are the worst teacher I ever had."

Although this couldn't possibly be true, Rocco reflected, he was surprised that the student thought he could do such a complete teacher evaluation in so short a period of time. So, Rocco grabbed a philosophy book, reread the chapter on logic, and in the end knew he had been right. Ultimately he felt pretty good about the whole episode.

"If I can turn each of those negative situations into a positive one," said Rocco, "why should we coddle the self-image of the students? They are more resilient than we are and will become better adults by facing some adversity along the way."

Rocco was indeed perceptive.

To see if the topic of self-esteem was as pervasive as Rocco thought, we looked it up on the Internet. A quick search yielded 928,000 mentions. There were sites such as the *National Association of Self-Esteem* (No, I'm not kidding!) and the *Self-Esteem Shop* (where you can buy books, posters, and games to make you feel better about yourself).

Rocco is always able to sum up a situation in a unique way, and he didn't disappoint this time as we approached the eighteenth green. "Don't dispense with your mind just to indulge your feelings. Any tool which helps you to cope with reality should have a special place in your toolbox."

"Whaaaat?" we said in unison.

31

PRANK

I know that bad habits are hard to break. I smoked cigarettes for ten years, from 1958 to 1968. During the last two years of that interval I tried to quit at least fifty times. I would buy a pack, smoke one, and throw the rest out the window of my moving vehicle. Sometimes, the following day I would go back and try to find the far-flung pack. On other occasions, I would flush the cirgarettes down the toilet. For a couple of months, when I taught at West High, I would bring one cigarette to school and think all morning about lunch-time and that first puff. Then, I quit smoking my own cigarettes completely. I became a very irritating person both because I was in withdrawal and because I started bumming cigarettes from any smoker unlucky enough to be in my vicinity. My most reliable source of cigarettes was my colleague Stan, who was a fantastic math teacher and one of my favorite people. He also had a marvelous sense of humor. I felt guilty bumming from Stan each day, but I couldn't help myself.

Because Stan was such a great guy and always treated me fairly, I felt a little guilty about the prank my colleague Steve and I pulled on him.

Between classes, the three of us would journey to a small lounge for a smoke, with Steve smoking his and Stan and I smoking Stan's. Stan had a favorite little chair that he always sat in because it had a little concave seat into which his butt fit perfectly. Since Steve was older, I respected his judgment. But I suspected he was up to no good. One day Steve instructed me to fill the indentation in Stan's chair with water. In spite of my misgivings, I did as instructed because I knew I could blame Steve for the joke if I got caught. I cringed when Stan came into the room and sat down. He casually lit up a cigarette and said to me, "Bob, is there some reason why you are not smoking today?" I did not answer, because I was struggling to suppress a laugh. Shortly afterward, Stan finished his smoke and leisurely left the room without another word. As he walked away from us, we could see the big, wet circular area on his rear end. Steve burst out laughing, and I just whimpered. After that incident, I never attempted to bum another cigarette from Stan, and shortly thereafter I quit completely.

My conscience has continued to bother me since that day, but I still laugh when I think about it.

Stan never mentioned the prank, but I'm sure he knew I was involved. He never offered me another cigarette.

32

MY MENTOR

At one time during my thirty-three years in education, I thought I might want to be an administrator. Compared to the everyday trials of the classroom, it looked like a "cushy" job. I reasoned that if I could get up from my desk and go for a walk or get a cup of coffee at any time, and tell people what to do, I might like it.

My idol at the time was Delbert, a laid-back administrator who had the uncanny ability to make people relax. He had a perpetual smile, was a real back-slapper, and could easily get along with anybody.

He was a dandy of sorts, always checking his image in a mirror or any other reflecting surface that was nearby to make sure he looked perfect.

One time during the early years, he invited me to ride with him to his hometown, Rome, N.Y. He promised that I would enjoy a wonderful pasta dinner with his parents. That was an offer I couldn't refuse. We did have a delicious meal, and I thoroughly enjoyed my visit with his folks.

On the ride back to Auburn that evening, I said, "Del, it was nice of you to ask me to your parents' home for fine wine, pleasant conversation, and a great meal."

"Bobby, there is only one reason I asked you to ride along with me, and that's because I knew it would be dark out on the ride home."

I nearly split a gut trying not to laugh.

One of the ways to learn about administrative duties and philosophy is through internships. If I could nail one down, I would surely improve my lot in life.

I approached Del and asked if he would be my mentor for an internship. He agreed, and I proceeded with the required paperwork.

During the internship he taught me many things, none of which helped me get a job as an administrator. One of the very valuable lessons was how to deal with the "cut slips" that arrive in the office during the general chaos of the opening days of a new school year. One day I walked into his office in a very frustrated mood. "Check out this stack of cut slips," I said. "I'm overwhelmed."

"Bobby boy, let me see that stack."

I gave him the two-inch thick stack. One by one, he went through the pile like this:

>"This kid's father is a doctor."—(This cut slip goes into the wastebasket.)
>
>"This kid's father is a lawyer."—(Definitely goes into the wastebasket.)
>
>"Joe Nobody."—(That's a keeper.)
>
>"This kid's father is on the School Board."—(Goes into the basket.)
>
>"This is my kid."—(You know where this cut slip goes.)
>
>"Barbara S."—(Nice looking. Into the basket.)

When Del was finished, the stack had been reduced to a very little pile. I said, "You can't do that, can you?"

"Bobby, when you are efficient and effective, you know intuitively which ones are mistakes; I'm just saving time."

"Did you learn that little trick in Education 601, some advanced education course?" I asked.

"No," he said chuckling, "I learned it from my mentor."

And that's how wisdom is passed from one generation of administrators to another. Since the whole situation now made sense to me, I never questioned Del's wisdom again. As I left his office, I said to myself, "I think I'm going to like this job."

Delbert ended his career as an effective, efficient, highly respected administrator. As testimony to this, there were many local people at his retirement party; in fact it resembled a mob summit.

"Is That Legal?"

BOOK V

COACHING

33

LUCKY

It really amazes me when people so easily attribute somebody else's success to luck. I agree that luck does play a role in such things as winning a lottery or guessing the right number between 1 and 100 during a guessing game. But most of the time, "luck" means hard work and personal sacrifice, whether it is academic, athletic or otherwise.

The journey and effort a young person puts forth in this life can be very rewarding. I am reminded of that "lucky" Janet Evans. Evans, the former Olympian, won several gold medals in swimming. Although she practiced twice a day, at 5 A.M., before she went to school and then again after school, several people said she was "lucky." Have you noticed that the harder you work, the luckier you get?

During my cross-country coaching days, we had two girls who were as lucky as Janet Evans.

Denise went on to win ten New York State championships in track and field and cross-country. She worked obsessively at practice, displayed great self-discipline, and won a full scholarship to the University of Kentucky.

Jenny was out of the same mold as Denise, eventually winning four New York State championships. Her reward was a full ride to Penn State.

Those coaching days were memorable for me. The 1986 cross-country team won the NYS Class A championship and the Federation Meet championship.

The Class A race was pure torture for me. It was about three minutes to "post" and our girls were nowhere in sight. "Al," I said, "Where are the girls? We are going to miss the start of the race." By this time I was hyperventilating and a potential heart attack dominated my thoughts. Al was nominally my assistant, but he was really like a co-coach.

"Don't worry, Coach," he said, as he pointed to the portable "johns" at the top of a nearby hill. "They will make it." I should have guessed where they were, because they were always nervous before a race and it was not unusual for them to need to go to the bathroom. As a matter of fact, I even felt the urge myself. Al was right, as usual. The girls even had time to spare as they showed up one minute prior to the start of the race.

Cross-country coaches need tough kids who can run 3.1 miles and cross the finish line with nothing left but willpower. I'll never forget the sight of one willowy freshman limping as she came out of the hills of Van Cortlandt Park in the Bronx, N.Y., the site of the 1986 Federation Meet. With tears in her eyes and in obvious pain, she refused to give up and finished the race on willpower alone. The image of her pain and determination is permanently etched in my mind.

The 1988 cross-country team won a "triple crown:"

New York State Class A Championship.

New York State Federation Meet Championship.

Eastern States Championship.

The 1988 Class A site was picturesque Lake Placid on a cold, snowy, windy day in late fall. The girls wore tights as their cold-weather garments. This gave them a sleek, streamlined appearance. I thought they looked "cool." The outcome of the race was determined by a tiebreaker rule. We were tied with Saratoga, but since our sixth girl beat their sixth girl, we were awarded the victory.

Laura, one of the tough starting seven, was always trying to find ways to liven things up. On the trip to Lake Placid, she would periodically utter a witticism that made us laugh and lessened our anxiety as we worried about the big race. On the trip home she played a Whitney Houston song, "One Moment in Time," over and over the entire way. I can still hear it. We had our moments, in 1986 and 1988. Personally, I hear another song as well—"Thanks for the Memories."

From humble beginnings with just one girl, Wendy, who trained with the boys, wore bells on her shoes, and helped us recruit other girls, we evolved into state champs within six years.

I considered myself fortunate to have had those two amazing teams. Al and I were also a good team. I used to kiddingly tell him that he was the brawn, while I was the brain of the team.

Sooner or later, though, all good things must end. The job had been highly rewarding, but it was also physically and mentally taxing. Knowing that the kids were in good hands with Al as their coach, I called it quits after the 1988 outdoor track season.

Since then the chest pains have disappeared and my blood pressure has returned to normal.

I was a lucky man to have had such good experiences.

I was also lucky to have survived those experiences.

1986 Champs

1988 Champs

34

HORMONES AND GEOMETRY

Parents, teacher, counselors, and others are always looking for outlets for teen-agers to constructively release hormone-rage.

We all learned in basic biology that humankind is differentiated from lower organisms by its superior cerebral development that often allows humans to brilliantly manipulate objects, remember, create, think, reason and speak languages. And yet, from the halls of congress to the churches and temples, the hormones rage. From the police department to the doctor's office, the hormones rage. And especially in the high school classrooms, the "basic instinct" struggles for control.

The best we can do, then, is to provide a temporary diversion for our teen-agers. One such diversion is athletics. Playing sports helps athletes alleviate the perpetual "hormone-rage" that accompanies adolescence. Hormonal influence is the primary guide for the daily activities of most high school students. Certainly everyone

211

would agree that hormones are wonderful little molecules, but they work best at the proper time and in the proper place. Unfortunately a hormone can usually outrun a moral value any day of the week. I have often thought that it would be wonderful if my students could check their hormones in at the door of my classroom, like checking one's coat at a restaurant. I can imagine the true magic that would occur as I derive the quadratic formula in math or discuss the mysteries of the Krebs cycle in biology, with no boy-girl distractions. But alas, this is only fantasy, and not nature's way.

If you remember proofs in geometry, the "given" is composed of premises and is accepted as the absolute truth. Then, usually through deductive reasoning, other truths are proven. It is a "given" that the daily activities of teen-agers are primarily influenced by hormones. Every waking moment is hormone-related. "Do I look good today? Will he notice me?"—these are dominating thoughts of adolescent girls. Boys have similar thoughts.

Let me tell you the story about Kathi and Bill.

Kathi and Bill were two members of my track team. The very first week of practice Kathi showed up on Monday and

Tuesday, but I didn't see her again till Friday. "Kathi," I said, "where were you Wednesday and Thursday?"

"You mean we have to practice every day?" she said innocently. After Friday's practice, Kathi and I had a little heart-to-heart to discuss and clarify team rules. I tried not to be preachy, but I did get my point across because subsequently she was a model athlete and an asset to the team.

Bill, a tall stripling, a gregarious lad, was one of three identical brothers (the P triplets, as we called them). He and his brothers, David and Pat, attained celebrity status at our school. Each was an exceptional runner, and it was always exciting to watch them race. Our cross-country meets were also fun, because we had a great boys' team and there was always speculation as to the order of finish of the P's. Questions like, "Who won?" or "That was Pat, wasn't it?" were frequent.

Although they were very hard working, dedicated athletes, occasionally one of them would try to get out of doing certain tough workouts. Sometimes their methods for doing this were quite creative. One time we were "running hills," a very grueling activity. David, or was it Pat, said, "Coach, I have a pain."

"Where's your pain?" I asked.

"Well Coach, what side is the appendix on?"

"The right side," I responded.

"That's where my pain is, Coach."

"Nice try; get back on those hills," I commanded.

As he headed back to the hills, he looked back over his shoulder and smiled.

Bill and David continue to excel athletically. They are internationally known triathletes, among the elite in the sport. The federal government employs Pat, the intellectual.

During practice, Kathi and Bill had an unusual way of getting from point A to point B. They often took a circuitous route that involved an exploratory detour to point C, an area hidden behind a big oak tree. When they finally reappeared, they were always a few minutes late rejoining the group. I knew that co-ed practice sessions were going to create problems, given the chemistry of teen-agers, but when I objected to the policy, I was outvoted by the administration. "We must stay current with the philosophy of the day," they said.

Kathi was in my geometry class. One day in class I tried to get Kathi to understand that the shortest distance between two points was on a straight line. During a moment of inspiration, I cleverly seized the opportunity to connect subject matter with real life. "Kathi," I said, "do you realize that when I instruct you at practice to go directly from point A to point B, and you frequently include point C, which is located behind that big oak tree, you are traveling a longer distance? By traveling a longer distance, you are therefore late rejoining the group."

She looked straight at me with a twinkle in her eye and a smile on her face. "That's not why I'm late, Mr. Cal," she said. I knew she wanted me to ask for an explanation, but I never did. I am amused by the fact that while I tried to relate book learning to real life, I was outsmarted by a teen-ager.

Today, I frequently see Kathi around town and she always mentions that teaching moment, with that same smile on her face. I still haven't asked her for an explanation.

Anne was Kathi's teammate on the track team, and our team captain. "I guess I'll go out tonight and hunt up some action," I heard her utter one day as I was making my way to practice. She had not seen me approach because she and Kathi were deeply involved in discussing their social life, and a small equipment shed temporarily hid me from her view. Anne, a high quality intellectual, was cotton-mouthed and at a loss for words when I asked her the next day how the "action" was.

Since I discovered that I could learn a lot from behind that shed, it became one of my favorite stopping places. The kids thought I was clairvoyant.

I try to keep adolescent behavior in perspective, because I, too, was an adolescent. I remember one "testosterone-moment" from my youth that had an athletic component. During my junior year of high school track, several teammates and I were caught red-handed peeking into the girls' locker/shower room. Unfortunately, we were caught before we could see the good parts. Like today's youth, whenever the opportunity presented itself, we behaved like rascals.

"Is It Safe To Come Out Yet?"

35

THE STAR THAT MOONED

As our girls' track team bus was leaving Henninger High School in Syracuse, after we had been soundly defeated, the girls were in a somber and depressing mood; fortunately, that mood turned out to be only temporary.

Suddenly, the Henninger coach yelled that one of my girls was "mooning" her team from the back window of the bus. The girl apparently thought it was her responsibility to teach some biology to her teammates as well as to her opponents. Without turning my head I said, "O.K., Kathy, put it away." Being the good coach that I was, I always looked the other way when Kathy was up to something, because she was one of our stars. Besides, a little "mooning" never hurt anybody and it did bring a lot of levity to our potentially gloomy ride home.

When Kathy did the same thing the following week, I asked her why the repeat performance. She said, "Mr. Cal, you said that repetition was the best way to get good at something, and I think I can be good at this."

"Don't do it again, Kathy. Do I have to repeat myself?"

"Only if you want to get good at it, Coach," she replied.

My mouth opened but no words came out. Once again I was foiled by a teen-ager.

I'm hoping that Kathy and her good buddy Leigh visit me soon to "shoot the breeze" and reminisce. The last time they came over, Leigh showed me the ankle tattoo she got when she was in her early twenties. I want to show them the rose tattoo I got when I turned sixty.

36

FORGETFULNESS

It really bothers me when kids make fun of my physical appearance. One time I went to the aid of a female hall monitor who was having a tough time with a brawny boy. He said to me: "Don't bother me, you fat, old man." When he started to walk away, I commanded him to stop, but of course he didn't.

Wow! I was verbally abused and suffered age discrimination and insubordination in less than thirty seconds. But, the part that bothered me the most was the "fat" part, because once again I was on a diet that apparently wasn't working.

When I got thinking about the word "old" that he used to describe me, I began to think once again about an event that occurred during my days of coaching girls' track. After teaching and coaching for a lot of years, I sometimes became forgetful.

One Saturday we were preparing to go to the New York State Indoor Track and Field Championships at Barton Hall

221

on the Cornell University campus. The team was to depart from the Auburn YMCA. I parked my car, on a diagonal, on the side of the street opposite the team bus. As I got out of the car I left the door open in anticipation of quickly returning. I opened the trunk to get the medicine kit and other essentials, herded the girls onto the bus, and gave the order to depart for Ithaca.

About thirty minutes later, halfway to our destination, I was horrified to realize that I had left the door open, the trunk lid up, and the engine running. Although I began to sweat, nobody noticed. After arriving at Barton Hall, I immediately called home. "Barb," I said, "I'm trying a little experiment. Would you go down to the YMCA and see if my car is still there?"

"What do you mean?" my wife said.

"Well, I left the driver's side door open and the trunk up and the motor running. I'm doing a study to see if people are honest." She hung up the phone without saying another word.

But I was right; people in Auburn are honest.

This condition, forgetfulness, might be infectious, and I may have infected others. One time during Regents exam week, four other teachers and I piled into Betty D's car and went to Webster's for lunch. After lunch, we found that the car doors were locked and the motor was running. The policeman who came to our rescue some 30 minutes later was a former student of mine who hadn't done very well in my class. He must have thought that it was my car or that Betty was "guilty by association" with me, because by the wide grin on his face and the I-guess-I'll-take-my-time-attitude, I knew that it was get-even time.

"Cornell, Here We Come!"

37

CELEBRITY

Coaches have to keep their perspective as well as their sense of humor intact for the many situations that arise. Each day brought new surprises.

It was things like the story of "Cletus" that made participating in athletics worthwhile.

Surprise was often fun—maybe not for the athlete involved, but certainly for the observer.

Cletus was one of the sprinters on our track team. If he had had a crystal ball, he probably wouldn't have run a particular race that day. He must have dressed quickly in order to be on time to catch the bus for one of our meets. Apparently he forgot to include his athletic supporter in his race gear. His forgetfulness became obvious when he won the 100-meter dash by a head, which was clearly visible to many of the spectators.

Cletus had the courage to endure the inevitable kidding that occurred, and he actually became somewhat of a celebrity.

Speaking of celebrity, I am reminded of Luigi, a real character who introduced a new concept to high school football. He was small for the position that he played, so he came up with some innovative ways to compensate. From his position at defensive nose-guard, he was adept at surprising friend and foe. Any time there was a pileup, and Luigi was among the bodies, he would leave teeth marks in somebody's leg. Usually the victim was an opposing player, but not always.

Luigi was one tough hombre.

"Just Like Filet!

38

THE SPECIALIST

Dickie was a 220-yard specialist on my track team. He was awesome in any short sprint and was a valuable member of the 880-yard relay team. I had many strategies to share with Dickie, because I had run the 220-yard dash during my high school days. Usually just before his race I would simply say, "Dickie, when the gun goes off, run like hell." It worked most of the time.

One time, because of a sudden injury to one of my other runners, I needed a body to run the 440-yard dash on a cool and windy day. I talked Dickie into filling in. I have forgotten what I promised him as an inducement, but before I had a chance to give him crucial instructions on how to run this grueling race, he had to take his place at the starting line. When the starter's gun went off, Dickie must have thought he was running the 220-yard dash, because he took off like a rocket. I remember yelling, "Oh no; slow down, Dickie!" The more I yelled, the faster he ran. At the 220-yard mark, he was literally 30 yards ahead of the rest of the field. Then he "hit the wall." He had exhausted every bit of energy in his body in a few blazing seconds. He had literally nothing left. He stumbled across the finish line dead last, coughing, choking, wheezing, and crying over and over, "Never again. Never again."

I helped him off the track, fearing that he might collapse right there.

"Dickie, why didn't you slow down when I yelled to you," I asked.

"Coach," he said when he could finally speak, "the wind was really tough on the backstretch. All I heard was your yelling and I thought you wanted me to run faster."

Dickie is over forty-years-old now, and whenever I see him, we start to laugh simultaneously, and he always says, "Coach, you did try to kill me, didn't you?"

I just wink.

"I'm Running As Fast As I Can!"

39

COACH BILL

For me, it was a lot of fun and a great source of laughter being around Coach Bill. Bill, a physical education teacher, was a lankly, angular guy, an outstanding four-sport athlete in high school, who appeared at times to be all elbows. He and I coached football together for many years. Although his polestar was honor and integrity, he peppered it with an amazing sense of humor. I couldn't wait to get to practice each day to see what lunacy he would entertain us with. The good belly laughs I had were better than psychotherapy …and cheaper.

However, I often thought I was living a scene from the book *Catch-22* when I was with him.

One time he said, "Just remember, Bo, wherever you go, you take yourself."

I inquired, "But what if you're schizophrenic, Coach?"

"In that case, you'd be traveling with a crowd," he replied.

Whenever the opportunity presented itself, and he would make sure that it was often, Bill would talk proudly about his alma mater, Colgate University. One time he was telling me how beautiful the fall foliage was in Hamilton, N.Y., the site of Colgate. Then he asked me where I went to school.

"ACC," I said.

"Oh, the Atlantic Coast Conference has some great schools. Which one did you attend?"

I never bothered to explain that ACC was Auburn Community College (now Cayuga Community College or CCC), but I told him that there was a beautiful view of McDonald's from the back terrace of the school.

"That's nice," he said.

On an occasion when Bill gave me a ride to ACC, where I taught part-time, I said, "Bill, how do you like my alma mater?" He looked at me quizzically, but said not a word. He never broached the question again.

When Bill engaged you in conversation, sometimes you knew where you started, but you never knew where you were going to end up, and you could never be sure that the conversation had actually terminated. At other times there was usually no beginning and no ending, just a continuation. He could take you on the most circuitous of circuitous routes. Later, when you would reflect on what had transpired, you knew that there had to have been a conversation going on, but it all seemed so unreal, so dreamlike.

After 38 years of being a main player in public education, Bill called it a day. In preparation for his retirement party, where I was the emcee, I would write notes of things I wanted to say, sometimes at the oddest moments. One time, in a delicate moment, I said, "Oops, I've got to write that down."

"Write what down? Are you taking notes? Are you crazy?" my wife yelled.

"Just be yourself," I said, "don't move and I'll be right back." Needless to say, the house was silent and I had to cook my supper for the next two weeks.

The following story went over well at the party: Out of the blue, one day Bill asked, "Bo, what do we do on sweep-8?"

"Bill, you and I played football for Coach Dean forty years ago; what difference does it make now?"

"I was just wondering," he said.

As I walked away, I turned slowly and said, "Oh, by the way Bill, we block down on sweep-8." He smiled and gave me the thumbs up.

All heads in the audience nodded in unison, for they too had visited the twilight zone. You had to be careful, though, because if you weren't, you could get trapped in that little world where time and space have no meaning.

My wife finally softened and forgave me for the "delicate moment" event alluded to earlier when I told her about one of Bill's biggest fears. He feared that some day while walking down the street, he would see himself walking in the opposite direction. But, he was terrified by the possibility that he might say "hello."

Bill's retirement party was two and one-half hours of continual laughter. At the end, everyone was spent with that feel-good exhaustion.

More belly laughs—less psychotherapy.

"What Do We Want To Play Today?"

"Mine's Better Than Yours!"

241

40

FOOTBALL

For a football coach, it is very important that his players think of him as omniscient and omnipotent. That's the way we like it. However, the truth may be something altogether different, but the fiction allows the coach to show his charges that he is the boss and is to be obeyed without question. I devised a scheme to do just that.

On the first day of practice without pads, I picked the biggest player on the team to assist me in a drill of my own invention. "Angelo," I said to the 240-pound hulk, "I want you to assist me in a little demonstration of leg strength."

"O.K. Coach, but what I gotta do?" responded the trusting and affable freshman.

"Do you see that mound over there?" I said, as I pointed to an area about fifty meters away.

"Yes, Coach, I see it."

"I want you to run toward it at three-quarter speed, and pick up your pace as you approach its base. Then, I want you to run up its near side, spring off the top with great leg thrust, and land on the other side. Got it, Angelo?"

"Got it Coach."

The ground shook from the thundering footfalls of the gigantic Angelo as he motored toward the mound, accelerated at the base as instructed, ran up the side and performed a perfect thrust skyward. We heard a splash, followed by the unmistakable, agonized voice of Angelo crying-out "ooooh…shiiiit," coming from the far side of the mound. We ran to investigate. The boys on the team broke out in uproarious laughter as they viewed Angelo, on his butt, in the middle of the biggest puddle of water ever seen on that field. Angelo gazed dumbly at his teammates. Perplexed at first, a big grin spread across his face as he saw his teammates laughing, and then he slowly, heartily laughed himself. "Did I do good, Coach?" he said, after he had regained his composure.

"Yes Angelo, you did good," I said. I was filled with relief that he was O.K. For a long time afterward I was accused of a setup. In retrospect, had I known that the water was there I would have canceled the demonstration. Right!

When I saw Angelo and his dad walking toward us at practice the next day, I turned to Bill and said, "Bill, since you are the head coach and make the big bucks, I'll excuse myself while you deal with Angelo's father. Also Bill, I have to go to the bathroom."

While Angelo and his dad were approaching Coach, it was readily apparent that the older man dwarfed the boy. As I slithered away, I knew that Coach was uncomfortable and I felt his pain.

Coach made me run laps with the kids for the next five days, claiming that someone might suffer from heat exhaustion, since the temperature was in the 90-degree range. Someone nearly did—me.

To know Angelo, though, was to love him. During one game our opponent's passing attack was really killing us. What at first seemed like lunacy turned out to be a brilliant plan devised by Coach to slow down their passing game. "Angelo," he said, "I want you to go in and play middle linebacker and I want you to "blitz" the quarterback. But, I want you to start the blitz as soon as our opponents break from their huddle."

"O.K. Coach," said Angelo, as usual never questioning what we told him to do.

At that moment I thought Bill had taken leave of his senses. He smiled at me and said, "Bo, I know what you're thinking, but trust me on this one." Sure enough as the offensive team broke from its huddle, Angelo started his blitz. Precisely as the ball was snapped, Angelo reached the line of scrimmage. With all of his 240 pounds in the air, he flattened that quarterback for a seven-yard loss. Coach slyly winked at me, and from that day forward I, too, never questioned his decisions, because I realized that he was a defensive genius.

After the sack, Angelo ran off the field with his face lit up in a broad smile. "Did I do good, Coach?" he asked with anticipation.

"Splendid! Wonderful!" I said.

"Magnificent!" Bill chimed in.

Angelo's good buddy, "Choochoo," was our fullback. Choochoo was a clone of Angelo, but a good deal smaller at 190 pounds. He was extremely elusive and could be counted on to get, as the saying goes, "three yards and a cloud of dust" every time he ran up the middle.

The code for our plays was very simple. For example, a play like 32 meant that the 3 back was to run through the 2 hole. But Choochoo had difficulty remembering these simple codes. It got so bad that Bill and I devised a scheme just for him. In the huddle the quarterback would say, "Chooch, get ball, run." Choochoo would smile while each lineman realized that his assignment was to block the nearest defensive player (we called it "logic blocking"). Most of the time it worked because the defensive players couldn't decipher our blocking scheme, mainly because we didn't have one. However, when it didn't work, we had some horrific collisions.

The obvious rivalry between linemen and running backs, manifested by their witty and spirited conversation, was always music to my ears.

A burly tailback named Al and a huge lineman named Dale usually provided that music. Dale would say, "Al, did you notice that huge hole I opened for you?"

"What hole?" Al would reply. "I made you look good because of my great cut and elusive footwork off your burly hide."

And so it went, a playful repartee with neither player giving an inch.

One year we had a flankerback, John, who had all the qualities of a great player. He was intelligent, quick, fast, and very elusive; his slightly bowed legs gave him great balance and stability. John proved himself in practice and was going to be our starting flanker and the return man on punts. A few days before our opening game, he was involved in a punt-return drill that he had practiced many times before. By happenstance or fate, the ball hit him in the thumb, broke it, and effectively ended his football career.

In some twisted way, John maintained that I was his hero while at the same time he blamed me for his misfortune. "Coach, you should have prevented me from doing the punt-return drill," he forcefully said.

"John, how did I know that you were going to break your thumb?" I asked.

"Don't you remember Coach? You said that after ten years of teaching and coaching you were psychic."

"John, what I said was that after ten years of teaching and coaching I was psychotic."

"What's the difference?" he asked.

"How should I know? I'm just the waterboy," I responded.

Never one to be defeated by a temporary setback, John went on to star in track and field where he specialized in the long and triple jumps. He was the type of kid you really didn't coach, because he had the wisdom to teach himself, and that's the way he preferred it.

As a coach, I thought of myself as a keen evaluator of talent, but one incident in particular taught me that I had a lot to learn. Near the end of our JV season, I was watching a passing drill involving our ends and quarterbacks. On one particular pass, our quarterback threw the ball towards out tight end. The pass was high, but Bobby reached up with his left hand, tipped the ball, and caught it on the rebound in that same hand. Since I thought my eyes had deceived me, the next time it was Bobby's turn to receive a pass, I instructed the quarterback to throw the ball beyond his reach. Sure enough, Bobby caught it the same way.

"Bobby," I said, "I didn't know you had such great hands."

"Coach, they are the same hands I had when the season started."

"Touché, Bobby."

Part of the problem had been that Bobby rarely said two words. He simply went about effectively performing his blocking duties at tight end, and I had never specifically called a play in which he was to receive the pass.

I am sure I missed other talented kids as well, but I can't forget Bobby because whenever I see him these days, some thirty years later, he holds up his hands and smiles. Fortunately, for the next two years when Bobby was on the varsity team, his coach made good use of his exceptional talents.

"Ooooh…Shiiiiit!"

"Got It, Coach!"

41

STOP THE BLEEDING

One time during my football coaching days I experienced that feeling of being helpless to stop the "bleeding." I was the head junior varsity coach at the time and Bill was my assistant.

During the last game of that JV season, we were playing Cortland, and I thought the kids had been well prepared, but we were on the short end of a 21-0 half time score. I was so upset and embarrassed, I could hardly talk. So I asked Bill to rally the team by giving them a pep talk. He gave a poignant speech, dynamically and with great animation, about character, guts, teamwork, the Gipper, et cetera. The boys became so motivated and eager for combat that they stormed out of the locker room and played the second half like creatures possessed. The game turned into a war and the kids risked bodily injury for Coach. When it was over, the players were totally exhausted and emotionally drained, their faces a chalky pallor.

The final score was 42-0.

The following Monday, I resigned from coaching football and went into therapy, again.

Bill took a year off and went to England as an exchange teacher.

When he returned, I asked him how he had enjoyed his experience overseas.

"You know Bo," he said, "it was really great, and I met a woman over there whom I really liked. But, she couldn't dunk a basketball while going to her left, so I stopped seeing her."

I never asked Bill another question regarding his experiences in England.

42

I AM SAM

Once in a great while a coach comes across a young man or woman who is the model of what an athlete should be. That was Sam, a young lad who played guard for my freshman football team back in the late 1960s. Sam was supreme dedication, enthusiasm and character all rolled into one. He led by example and he didn't know the word "quit."

A perfect example of Sam's work ethic presented itself one day during freshman football practice. We were doing a dummy drill and I had told the kids to hit the dummies with their shoulders and "keep those legs moving." After starting the drill, Coach Bill and I must have become distracted for four or five minutes. By the time we realized that we had forgotten about the drill, all of the kids were lying on their bellies panting heavily from exhaustion, except for Sam. His legs were still churning and he had dug a hole about six inches deep in the soft turf.

During a moment of inspiration after practice Bill said, "Bo, bring a shovel to practice tomorrow; I have an idea." The next day Bill showed up with a seedling and I with my shovel. After I expanded the width and depth of the hole made by Sam, Bill planted the seedling to commemorate the event.

After thirty-five years, that seedling has grown into a mighty oak tree, and occasionally Bill, Sam and I visit that practice field from long ago to admire it and reminisce about old times.

"The Fruit Of My Labor."

BOOK VI
THE END

43

ATTENTION GETTERS

There were times during my teaching days when I needed to get the immediate attention of my students. I would use whatever means that were readily available— sometimes it was a waste basket and other times it was a missile.

There was on particular student who had stretched my patience to the limit. He was prone to fall asleep during my dynamic math class. One day he dozed off during an especially important lesson. I took aim at his position in the back of the room. The eraser missed Dan and hit the chalkboard behind him. He awoke with a startle, covered in dust from the board. His classmates chuckled and he turned a beautiful crimson.

At a meeting I attended recently, the guest speaker, who was the managing editor of a newspaper, turned out to be a former student of mine. Throughout his speech he kept making eye contact with me and strained to keep from laughing. Later he approached me. "Mr. Calimeri, do you remember the time you threw an eraser at me while I was sleeping in class and got chalk all over my sweater?"

"Dan, I remember it well and I can tell you unequivocally that there was no chalk on that eraser."

He roared with laughter.

Another time, I got more creative. With no other projectile handy, I resorted to my loafer-type shoe. I knew that the sight of a missile and the sound of it hitting the door would get the attention of my class. So, I let it fly. The door opened at about the same instant that the shoe hit it. The assistant principal who was coming to my room to do an unannounced evaluation just stood there with mouth agape. My shoe lay on the floor and was hidden behind a desk. I was balanced on one foot with my stockinged foot still in the air, and the kids were tottering between laughing hysterically and being bug-eyed in rapt attention. To this day, I am thankful that I didn't release my shoe two seconds later.

After the near miss, the shoe always stayed on my foot, except for my very last day of full-time teaching; I needed to do a final performance that I would remember as "the end." Having by now become proficient at launching missiles, I kicked my shoe one more time toward the door. This time the act was only partly spontaneous and doubly forceful. The shoe was still in mid-flight as the door swung open and the math department chairwoman appeared and....

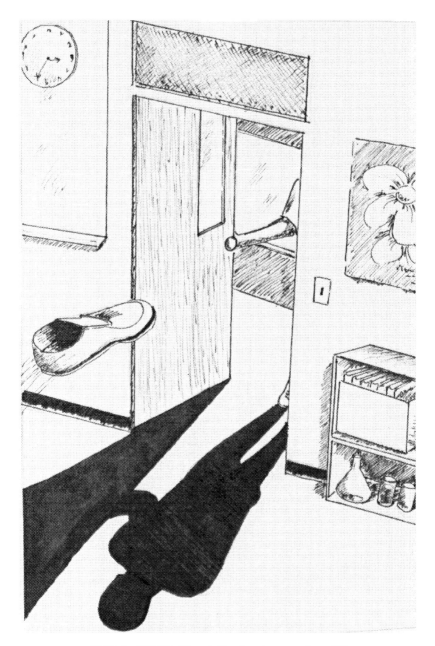

"This Will Get Their Attention!"

44

THE OLD MAN

When I was a kid, I loved to visit that old farm because it was way out there, far from the city. It had an old barn and lots of chickens and a few horses, too. But my greatest joy was when I saw the Old Man. I would always find him in his garden, the one place in the world he loved to be.

He would be bent over, doing what he loved to do. His hair was almost gone, but his handlebar mustache was perfect, as always. His leathery hands and face showed the wear and tear of his eighty years. His hoe was lying on the ground next to him; his shovel was in his hands. While engaging in a morning of toil, he would be sweating profusely in the summer heat.

I would sneak up on him in my combat crouch. When I was close enough to strike, he would say, without looking up from his toil, "Bobby, do you want to help Grandpa in the garden today?" Although I was five years old at the time, Grandpa and I enjoyed this little game. I could never figure out how he knew I was there.

Although that was nearly sixty years ago, I can still see the twinkle in Grandpa's eye when he said my name.

On the many occasions when I thought about my grandfather, I often wondered if my waning years would be as peaceful as his appeared to be. Since he lived most of his life in the country, occasionally going to the city to peddle fruits and vegetables from his horse-drawn wagon, his pace of life was slow and there appeared to be few calamities.

Since I have lived a more hectic life in the city, I generally finish every year by telling my students this: "Some day when you are walking the beach, and you see a little old man sitting in the sand carving a piece of wood, say hello, tell me who you are and how I know you and then tell me who *I* am."

That's just the way it is sometimes, the consummation of one's life.

As many of us know, there is a fine line between sanity and insanity. In order to know what sanity is, one needs to know what insanity is. I think I finally know the difference between the two. However, in case I slip a little, it may be O.K., because sometimes the *craziness* of the mind and the *craziness* of the world cancel each other out.

At present, though, my friends, but not all of them, say I am cheerful, centered and full of vim. This is good, because I worried that I was going to morph into a crotchety, cantankerous old fuddy-duddy.

This, then, is the end of the beginning of my literary career, or more likely the beginning of the end.

I hope you have enjoyed the journey.

"I've Got Him Now!"

"Do You Know Who I Am?"

Printed in the United States
20509LVS00006B/52-279